A **PEACE**

LOOK IN MY MIRROR

SANDY RODGERS

Sandy Rodgers Ministries provides you
with empowering words to
Awaken your Potential and Possibility
Awaken Endless Power
Discover Your Unlimited Opportunities!!

BALBOA.
PRESS
A DIVISION OF HAY HOUSE

Copyright © 2016 Sandy Rodgers.

Editor: William Saafir
Graphic Designer: Bobby Smith
Cover Design: Chuck Spady, OCD-Studios.com
Cover Photography: Carline Richardson

All rights reserved. No part of this book may be used or reproduced by any means, graphic, electronic, or mechanical, including photocopying, recording, taping or by any information storage retrieval system without the written permission of the author except in the case of brief quotations embodied in critical articles and reviews.

Balboa Press books may be ordered through booksellers or by contacting:

Balboa Press
A Division of Hay House
1663 Liberty Drive
Bloomington, IN 47403
www.balboapress.com
1 (877) 407-4847

Because of the dynamic nature of the Internet, any web addresses or links contained in this book may have changed since publication and may no longer be valid. The views expressed in this work are solely those of the author and do not necessarily reflect the views of the publisher, and the publisher hereby disclaims any responsibility for them.

Any people depicted in stock imagery provided by Thinkstock are models, and such images are being used for illustrative purposes only.
Certain stock imagery © Thinkstock.

ISBN: 978-1-5043-6463-8 (sc)
ISBN: 978-1-5043-6492-8 (e)
ISBN: 978-1-5043-6464-5 (h)

Library of Congress Control Number: 2016902752

Print information available on the last page.

Balboa Press rev. date: 09/10/2016

As for African American women, our mirror of beauty and acceptance has long been smashed into a million pieces, not just cracked .... *Sandy Rodgers*

CONTENTS

A Peace of Heaven vii
Sandy Rodgers's Personal Declaration ix
Dedication.. xiii
Introduction xv

Stage 1   Self-Acceptance 1
Stage 2   Sitting.. 23
Stage 3   Remembering 31
Stage 4   Releasing.. 45
Stage 5   Happiness 51
Stage 6   My Mirror 59
Stage 7   Masculine 65
Stage 8   What Is Beauty? 77
Final Stage Positive Spiritual Upliftment 91

Acknowledgements 111

A PEACE OF HEAVEN

A subsidiary of Sandy Rodgers Ministries

- -

    P   Positive

    E   Enthusiastic

    A   Affirming

    C   Confident

    E   Energy/Essence

SANDY RODGERS'S PERSONAL DECLARATION

My purpose is to live the true definition of unconditional LOVE of the Infinite Source. In my moving about this Universe and as I Love on people appearing on my path, I am reminded that many do not know how to do this. For many, a display of affection is almost foreign to them or reminds them of a negative experience so they are cautious. Lack of a positive example is often to blame. My Intention is to help anyone that would receive my messages of Healing, Wholeness, Restoration, Forgiveness and LOVE to live life more completely! And in so doing I have and am accomplishing my work here on Mother Earth. I am excited about reaching the masses worldwide; to continue building my international audiences and witnessing the transformation of all those I work with!!

My intention is that you will be blessed with the reading of this writing. May you have the opportunity to Look in your mirror and be blessed, happy and satisfied. If the images you see are somehow currently distorted may there be a word, a phrase or a story to help guide you to the reality that you are indeed worthy of unconditional love and acceptance. You are Love and are Loveable. You are made whole and complete in the undeniable Love of God. You are made perfect, in human form, by The Most High. You are the Light of this world.

I pray for all humans to receive this truth of who they are. May there be a sudden spark that ignites the spirit within you. My prayer is you accept without doubt or disbelief that you are an unrepeatable Miracle. And you know with certainty that God makes no mistakes nor humans with flaws. We are each unique in our body form, whatever that may happen to look like. Our uniqueness is God's way of blessing us with our individual finger print, so to speak. We are made from UNCONDITIONAL LOVE and we cannot argue that. Many were never born, many have transitioned before us. So I ask you to accept the Miracle of your BE-ing with ease and joy.

There is only ONE YOU!!

As for African American women, our mirror of beauty and acceptance has long been smashed into a million pieces, not just cracked......Sandy Rodgers

DEDICATION

This book is written to help remind each of us of our connection to Source. The One Source of all creation. The Master Source of Civilization and the Universe knows the Beauty inside of you. The Energy of all living things carefully placed the very substances of life in you to exist with ease on this planet Earth.

The Most High God has created us perfectly just as we are. In our creation we are crafted with everything we require to be the abundant living beings that we are.

Look In My Mirror is dedicated to the Beauty and Possibilities of all females, the mothers of all Civilization since the very beginning of time. We are Ladies of Love, Women of Wonder.

We must learn to look into our mirrors with complete abandon as to what has been said to us in the past and trust that we are sufficient, loving, lovable, worthy humans. We are created 'in the image and after the likeness' of the Holy Creator of all things.

To the men I offer the same message of wholeness. You are perfect and complete. You are strength and wisdom. Be proud as you gaze into the reflection in your mirror. Your creation is masterful and unrepeatable. You are unique and genuine. You are Love, lovable and loving,

"Trust God in me. God is my potential." ... Rev. Sandy Rodgers

INTRODUCTION

A Peace of Heaven book series serves as a Wholistic answer to the many facets of daily living.

What began as a weekly class has evolved into this series of writings, which seeks to answer the various questions that repeated themselves within each class. When we attempt to box-in, limit or control what we think, feel or believe to be the summation turns out to be only the beginning. At least that's how it continued to reveal itself to us with every class. So our quest became to begin with a thorough understanding of the topic at large. We defined, then re-defined what we had just defined. We only stopped once we reached a mutual agreement as to what the topic really was. This may sound long and tedious, yet it was so worth the time and effort. What we discovered to be true was often times we assumedly begin a conversation believing all are on the same wave length. Sometimes basic words need to be defined because there may exist varying degrees of understanding for that particular word. Words get their meaning and have an impact on our lives dependent upon on our unique experiences in life. We must honor this within each person we relate and have conversation with. For truly no one will ever think exactly the same as we do, no one!

We have a tendency to reduce our human needs to a few categories such as emotional, physical and mental. Yet there are so many more aspects to our lives. There are also spiritual, nutritional and energy issues to discuss. Topics of family and community are indeed worthy of conversation. We found throughout the Wholistic Wellness classes that our survival depends a lot on being able to respond to all of the issues that surfaced, even when they did not match the topic of the day. We allowed life to unfold as it would without any forcing on our parts. We refused the idea that we had to stay 'on task' of the original topic. Instead, we honored what came up and out in terms of discussion matter.

So being flexible in understanding, when serving others, require attention and questioning to make sure the inquiry was answered to the person's satisfaction. Therefore, the various writings that will comprise each book will offer alternative views in addressing the main topic.

One's daily journey consist of reflection; self-talk; inner inspiration; healthy relationships; respecting and honoring all of humanity; our views on the outer world; self-motivation and self-love. How we use these dimensions are reflective of our inner dialog and values.

The activities that we find ourselves in on a day to day basis such as working, sleeping, driving, eating, or talking are minor things compared to the real substance of life. We are more than any one of those things or the summation of all those things combined. We are true treasures. We are whoever we declare ourselves to be. The ending of your 'I am" statements, tells the world who you have chosen to be. 'I am' is a powerful phrase, please ensure you are using it wisely.

Our power lies in our spoken words; the tongue forecasts the future with exactness. We think the thought, then speak the thought and it happens. Maybe not immediately, yet eventually it appears. When we choose thoughts and words that reflect the royalty of our Be-ing, we manifest abundance in our lives. I AM ABUNDANCE is a powerful thought and phrase to use often during the day.

The abundance is not necessarily financial; the abundance is in the understanding of how rich we are, pure and simple. We need not add anything to us to be worthy. We are worthy by definition of our being. We are worthy because we are alive. We are worthy because our Creator deemed us so.

We are complex creatures and as such, we must review all aspects of who we are. The answer to our survival and self-understanding is simple; we must honor our physical creation and our spiritual being. The Most High God respects and honors us in pure totality.

The series 'A Peace Of Heaven' seeks to help bring the best of you out and into full view. We will look into various subjects/topics to shine light on possible new ways of looking at a situation. As Muhammad Ali said, *"He who is not courageous enough to take risks will accomplish nothing in life."*

There is never one 'standard' course of action for anyone to take. There are always different roads to take; we always have choices and options. We each are unique expressions. We hold our own answers to life within us. To honor that individual, which is YOU, is so vital. Buddha would advise you, *"Do not overrate what you have received, nor envy others. He who envies others does not obtain peace of mind."*

May you be blessed with the reading; the intention is to give you a glimpse into **'A Peace of Heaven'**. The place or point of a higher consciousness that imparts Joy into every activity you engage in. The Heaven of this earth that resides in your heart and pours out into the Universe from you to bless and enrich you and those around you.

Look In My Mirror is a compilation of selected writings from the personal library of #1 *Amazon* Best Selling Author Sandy Rodgers. Understanding the importance of self-love as the first step to all healing, *Look In My Mirror* delivers a number of writings to emphasize and express this point.

Self-love allows you to look into your mirror with complete acceptance. Self-love connects you to the One Source of all life. Whatever name or term you use to describe that Life Force Energy is sufficient unto itself. Even if you do not recognize or honor a Higher Power or Intelligence, please feel free enough to read and enjoy the messages this book offers.

With much Love and Gratitude to you the reader.

Sandy Rodgers

STAGE 1

Self-Acceptance

BEAUTY IS IN THE EYE OF THE BEHOLDER
DO YOU LOVE WHO YOU ARE?

I am an elder with tremendous pride of who I am. I have somehow managed to defy/deflect the typical labels and descriptions that people would normally place on others. I have seen and been witness to numerous history making events in my short life; Civil Rights Movement, segregation, racial wars, inner city riots, our initial voyage into space, new technology – computers, evolution of music from vinyl records (78, 33 1/3 and 45 speeds) to 8 track to MP3, the invention of the mobile/cell phone and the election of the United States' first African American President, Barak Obama.

The 1930's represented a rather peculiar time in history. The systematic process of the creation of slavery and the belief that the slaves were inferior worked to keep people of Africa in line. People of color were shaken to their core of belief and understanding about who they were. Many had accepted the reality of their physical uniqueness being 'Ugly', 'Weird', 'Strange' or something to be ashamed of. This group was called by many derogatory names such 'Tar baby', 'ink spot', 'stayed in the oven too long' etc. the humiliation was endless. Many believed that their intelligence was inferior to the so-called majority class of citizens, the whites, the Europeans. The land was inhibited by the Indian who are the only true Americans. These whites were just as foreign to the land as were the people of color, of African descent. The whites did an effective campaign to remove the royal blood they had robbed from Africa. The families were divided, native rituals were forced to be abandoned and any connection to the language that was proudly spoken was met with harsh treatment including death. The people were bought and sold as property same as with cattle and other animals. This slavery business robbed the innocent essence of a great people.

The 1930's referred to as Post slavery was a period when people awakened from the dream/nightmare of slavery to find themselves still enslaved. They were enslaved mentally, and not prepared for their new reality labeled 'freedom'. It was a time of violence because for many that was the only way to verbalize and demonstrate their feelings. They were confused, angry and simply wanted to be accepted as a whole people. The laws that referred to these once royal people as 2/3 of a person. Violence was how they reached the shores of America. Violence was how they were raped from their native land of Africa. Violence was what kept the slave trade active for as long as it did. Violence was the order of the day to maintain this so-called civilization in order. Killings, lynching, murders, rape, brutality at its worst. This was the way of life for the new America and its population of people of color.

How did these individuals find their way in this new America? How did they overcome such a horrific existence? Who was bold enough to come to the aide and offer positive assistance? Many were mentally drained and physically wiped out. Many looked for new lands in this place called the United States of America to escape the horrors of this condition of living called slavery. Some simply did not make it. Some were forever lost in finding their way. Many held unto the lies that were hand-fed to them about their worth and value to society. My parents, for instance, were among the so-called lucky ones to escape the southern portion of the states, 'The South'.

But how did being only a generation away from the plantation fields of slavery affect them, how were they raised to think about themselves, what did it mean to them and their self-description? Both my paternal and maternal grandparents worked the slave plantation fields in Louisiana. My paternal grandfather also worked the plantation fields in Alabama. It's not been easy to get the answers to these questions from my parents nor other elders that were raised in this same time period. I would often be told not to bring such subjects up, to leave well enough alone. In other words, they did not want to 'remember' the truth of their past lives. Truth never dies, sometimes it is hidden from plain sight for a generation, but never too far away. Did they still believe they were 'ugly' and 'unworthy'?

As I was coming of age in the 1960's I proudly wore a magnificent afro hairstyle. I loved it and the pride in my heritage that it represented. I was sassy, bold, confident and elegant with displaying the natural beauty in the curls, the kinks and the waves of my natural hair. The same kinks that I paraded around, blacks had gone to great lengths to remove by straightening, with lye, or other harsh and damaging chemical treatments on their hair for years. The kinks were a symbol of ugly to most of my elders back then. Somehow the act of this new younger generation of wearing what was called 'afros' was a summons to remember the days of self-hatred. They did not call it that, they were still attempting to figure out their place in life. Younger in their lives they were unable to have discussions about such things. They were raised in the 'do as I say' generation, 'respect your elders'. The respect meant you did NOT ask questions, you simply obeyed the rules without any deviations. For my grandparents would definitely halt any such conversations. I may have been angry but never confused about my black beauty. How can I give to someone else the right to define me? My ancestors may have thought this, but were never able to voice it.

I had chosen to remain in a place that did not look to nor need others approval or opinion of me to decide the style of my choice. My validation would come from me and me only. My family strongly protested my desire or need to wear my hair 'nappy', what a shame and disgrace to the community I had become. Did I not realize how far we had come for me to now regress the race back multiple years, centuries, generations single handily? Ha! For clarification, Nappy is the language used to describe the nature of my natural hair texture, being of African descent. The word is intended to be negative and not a compliment. Like the young children's nursery rhythm suggests, 'Sticks and stones may break my bones, but names will never hurt me.' I wore my 'nappy' hair proudly.

Did I not care that I could be labeled as 'militant'? What about being peaceful like Martin Luther King Jr. who preached peace all over the nation? So many were offended by what was merely a display of my natural beauty. I was not being rebellious; I was being prideful of my rich heritage. And in fact this was a 'peaceful demonstration' of my right to certain privileges as a human being. Why was my action such a problem for the tribe? I could never quite understand why I got all the negative treatment. My spirit seemed to be set free by the display of wearing my hair in a nappy, natural state!

The late 1960's were my self-discovery years. The teenage years are always a time of exploration. I willingly served with community empowerment organizations through active participation, the focus was one of improvement. Prior to college I had served the Watts community and its residents with time and labor to improve the conditions for the elderly residents and to bring pride back to the citizens. So I had prepared myself to enter into this next phase of life. I had worked diligently to earn a full scholarship to a prestigious University. My choice was UCI – University of California at Irvine.

Throughout my school years, beginning with elementary I was a serious and studious learner. As I entered college, I was a member of the initial BSU (Black Student Union) movement. This was the first entrance of black students for the University of California systems back in the late 1960's. What a time to be alive as a young Black person, a Negro, a colored, an African American. What a shock to the lighter complexioned individuals that had been the sole residents of these colleges. We were all prideful of our ancestry. As James Brown sung his song "I'm Black and I'm Proud' we were convinced of our rightful status of a deserving human being. Some were active Black Panthers who wore dashikis (African clothing worn by men), colorful African attire by the females and used intentional hand gestures of pride. Eager and intelligent black youngsters entered into the University of California system.

"...Yet The Creator was so purposeful in providing separate identity to each of us."

I looked forward to receiving my college education. Excited about my future and what this college education would and could do for me and my family. I had prepared myself all through the earlier years of schooling. I took the hardest, most advanced and challenging classes in every subject. I too wanted to attain to my highest position in life. I was repeatedly told that the only way to get there was by a college education. So dutifully I mastered each subject with pride.

Yet when I finally headed off to obtain this wonderful experience I was met with violence and threats of forcefulness by members of the majority's clan, they were called them KKK. Klu Klux Klan. Here in beautiful southern California I would discover racism and hatred of the worst kind. My life was suddenly placed in jeopardy. This is the landscape: Older white men sitting on crates and milk barrels outside the local convenience store where all UCI students purchased food, yelling obscenities at us with every chance they had. The us, I am speaking of, is the black students that were now enrolled and a part of UCI. Why is this happening is the question we kept asking? Why can't we get the education we came here to obtain? Instead we were greeted with vulgarities and cruel treatment by the elders of this new community. Screaming they were **'going to lynch them some niggers!' They would be chewing tobacco and spitting it out on the ground in our pathway.** This was California not someplace in the Deep South. I was both terrorized and traumatized. Had nightmares for a very long time, this was some scary stuff for a young adult.

My family history is rooted deep in the South. Both my father and mother were born and raised in Louisiana. Most of my growing up years were spent visiting with my relatives in Louisiana during the summer months each year. The South and its racial discrimination and dangers were not uncommon to me. I had been warned plenty of times on how to act and react in certain situations. We were taught how to carry yourself in the presence of white people, in the south! Sounds strange even now as if we were travelling to some foreign place or something. Yet I had never received any disrespect or vulgarities towards me nor any of the other members of my family. We were always treated with respect and dignity. Yet there in sunny Southern California, supposedly a place of class and a higher echelon of folks is where I experienced hatred and racism. The experience was horrible to say the least.

These men that threatened the life of the young students were old, ugly white men, men of a lighter complexion than us, of European descent, they were European-American and we were African-American. They were fat with stomachs hanging over their belts, hanging low into their laps as they sat on the crates. The pants were too small around the waist and because they could not get their pants high upon the waist as they belonged, when they sat they showed the cracks of their behinds! We use to tease, between ourselves that is probably where the phrase 'cracker' came from! Anyway not all were fat. Some were tall and skinny with unshaven facial hair. They looked un-kept, unclean. Their faces were red with serious frowns set deeply upon them. Maybe this is what a devil looked like. For who could be so unkind to some young folks who are merely attempting to get an education? They were mean, evil, scary looking men and they frightened the daylights out of us young adults/teenagers.

Those were difficult years for blacks, especially those who wanted to get an education. There was simply too, too much violence for me to withstand. Trembling inside and out just to go make purchases at a community convenience store. My fellow students and new friends urged me to stay, yet I couldn't. Where is this land of opportunity that I learned about in school all along my primary educational years? Where is this place that my family urged me to attend? ….Where indeed? Were the people afraid of educated Blacks advancing beyond them? Were they simply ignorant and uneducated? Were they just that full of hatred and violence? So many questions for a young mind to wrestle with. Is the payoff worth the turmoil? Who will save me if I do encounter violence? Question after question plagued my mind.

I longed for a place of peace. At 18 I had already experienced the terrors of a riot, the Watts Riot of 1964 and now this at a college? This was yet another fight for blacks. The fight was not for something not due us, but a fight for equal access to life. I had earned a right to attend this University campus with all the other students of all races. UCI, University of California at Irvine, was not a foreign land that prohibited American citizens. No, it was less than a hundred miles from where I lived… where I had grown up. The inner city, then called 'the ghetto' of Watts California.

Perhaps at this point in my life, my hairstyle was a militant statement! Yet I was still okay with it and not willing to change nor compromise. My style was not a representation of hostility or anger. It was a show of pride in who I am/was. My origin is of African ancestry. I cannot overlook nor hide that fact of my life. Why were they still asking me to change to conform to what others thought of me?

Fast-forward with me, approximately 40 years through my time machine. I have worn so many, varying hairstyles mostly straightened styles during these years. I have worn every style imaginable. I wore it short, braided and permed; dyed and fried was the phrase back then. I became a hair model for several stylists. Became known for always sporting a new and different style that no one had ever seen before. I was a trendsetter. I never had a complaint...only ample compliments and praise.

In 2004, I chose to wear my hair in Dreadlocs. Dreadlocs are a natural braided African kinky, nappy hair style. With this style the hair has been allowed to grow in a 'locked' style. The hair is not combed through to untangle the knots or kinks. It is allowed to grow in its most natural state. Dreadlocs are similar to the style worn by Nefertiti and other female African Royalty. Oh how this upset the apple cart for real!! That is an old saying which means people were upset with me once again! Funny they thought I had become tamed! My Dad was so furious with me, I thought he was going to disown me as his baby girl. He did threaten to do just that if I did not come to my senses and wear my hair in a suitable style of a professional woman. But when I asked him what that looked like he could not answer me.

I explained to him what I had recently learned about the dangers of relaxing my hair with chemicals. The chemicals from permanent relaxers leave small amounts of residue on the brain each time they are applied. The chemicals go through the scalp to the inside– the brain. I asked him what he thought that might look like after years of abusing my scalp and hair follicles with chemicals. Not surprising he had no response. After several years, he finally stopped fighting me over my chosen hair-style of Dreadlocs. But it was his fight alone. I had made a conscious decision to wear this style. My nieces and nephews had been wearing their hair in dreadlocs for many years up to this point. I absolutely loved them and the freedom they exhibited. I was excited to be joining them with new hair style.

My hair grew longer than it had ever grown before. My Dreadlocs were absolutely stunning. They were beautiful. My hair grew to reach my waist. The problem I encountered was that because I had never worn or grown my hair that long it took some getting used to. Sometimes I would forget to move my hair from behind my back and shoulders as I drove my car. My hair would get caught behind my shoulders and when I turned my head I would pull the muscles in my neck! Ouch, that hurts. I was causing stress on my neck and shoulder muscles. My neck began to hurt so often that I had to take a serious look at what I was doing to contribute to this awful feeling. I asked myself what changes I can make to correct this pain I experienced.

My hair had never grown longer than shoulder length. That was only once just before I cut my hair off to begin the Dreadlocs phase. Funny while using the chemicals to relax and straighten my hair it never ever grew much. This was so much more than just merely changing my hair style. This decision literally changed my life. The locs were a spiritual journey for me. A journey of true definition and a personal proclamation of freedom. The experience was empowering and enriching. However, in the winter of 2010 my answer to the neck pain was I decided I would cut my locs off... that was **my** choice at that time.

I asked a dear friend my adopted God-daughter, Marlo Oliver, to do a semi-professional head shot session with me one Friday night. We had so much fun together. She had no idea what was to happen next. Actually neither did I. We both wore Dreadlocs. And often people thought we were mother and daughter. So I loved every minute of this time together. I changed clothing several times. We found additional spots where I could pose for extra shots. We used a massage table, the floor and several other locations for the pictures. We were extremely creative and having so much fun enjoying our time together. Lighting was adjusted and props added or removed. We had so much fun! This was a new adventure for us to explore together.

When I returned home later that same night, I cut all of my locs off, all by myself! I felt so liberated. It was another step in my spiritual journey. It was as if I were in a trance. The calling was to do something completely different. What I know to be sure is not everyone will allow themselves the opportunity to explore different looks or styles. Most people must go along with the modern media trends. I have always gone against the grain. I have always had independent thoughts of my own, which I acted upon purposefully. I believe that's why I was very successful as a clothing Designer... I was always creating the unexpected.

In 2011, what I found to be true is that some things, thoughts, attitudes and beliefs, just do not change. My mother told me how awful and ugly I looked with my nappy hair back in the 1960's! And why didn't I do something about it! Then my father took over in the 2000's when I chose to wear another natural look, dread locs. He pleaded and begged me not to go on with this my latest 'anti-establishment' act of being a rebel. I had not known him to go to such lengths to attempt to make me change something about me. He had always been very proud of his baby girl, but not this time. "Why would I dare walk around with my hair so nappy, I would never get a job or a husband!" He was so determined and adamant, in a way it tickled me but to tell the truth it really knocked me to the core of who I am and was. I thought he knew me better than to assume I was fighting against some beauty standard. I was simply 'being me' … as always!!

I thought she was stunningly BEAUTIFUL.

Fully embracing my beauty, I had to put some distance between me and my father. Here is a man I had become extremely close to during my development into adulthood. But, he drew the line and somewhere deep inside of me I just 'had to stand my ground'. There was no compromise to be had. My attempt was not to be some rebellious, angry black woman. I simply wanted the freedom to express myself in a natural way that I approved of and no one else. I did not seek outside validation because I did not want or need it. I was perfectly 'peace-filled' in my decision process. In my situation, my hair style took my dad back to a time he had chosen to forget! But there I stood, being proud of my African heritage!! It unsettled him to such a huge degree. I had never witnessed him so distraught over a situation before.

And yes my dad finally grew to love my hair, nappy and all. He was probably more proud of the fact that I could not or would not be deterred by him and his many ways to change my style. I always tell him I get my stubbornness from him! Plus I had grown my hair to unbelievable lengths. It was all the way down my back touching and caressing my waistline! Secretly my dad probably liked the idea that my hair was longer than it had ever been in my lifetime. The length of a woman's hair is a whole different story in and of itself, especially in the black or African American community!!

So when I met the absolutely most beautiful dark ebony baby I had seen in a very long time, I almost lost my sensibility. Her mother began making excuses as to why she, the baby, was wearing her hair in a natural style. I thought she was stunningly BEAUTIFUL. I asked the mother to never do that again. She sounded like my own mother from years back. Please do not make excuses or apologize for her natural beauty, I told her! This baby was Gorgeous, adorable smile and all! She was only five years old. Full of wonder and innocence. Was this the first time the mother spoke harshly about this baby's hair in her presence? How long had she been a witness to the less than positive words about her hair from her mother to another human being? Does this form of communicating have lasting effects on the little girl? Does it somehow relay that her look is less than acceptable or she is less pretty?

Actually, I wondered what she, the mother thought of me since my own hair was in a short natural style! I was wearing my dread locs again. I was at the beginning infant stages, in the first month or so. They were short, sassy locs. In my mind I'm wondering if she thinks my hairstyle affects my ability to satisfactorily perform the job she had hired me to do.

But even more puzzling to me was the fact that the mother being very well educated, dual degreed made what appeared to be foolish choices when it came to her own hair care. Due to tremendous abuse and neglect, using chemicals and wearing braids/extensions her hairline was about 2 to 3 inches away from its original location! Yes it had receded that much! Its distressing considering the fact that even with all the education she had, she would rather lose her hair than discontinue putting straightening concoctions in her tresses. Perhaps this is an act of not loving who she was totally.

I will not attempt to pass judgement here. What I see all too often is women of color wearing lengthy extensions of a woman with a different nationality than theirs. The texture is not the same. The question I ask is, are women today self-identifying with the artificial hair as being a sign of beauty while they look upon themselves as ugly when handling their own natural hair? Has the beauty industry tricked all females into believing they need those hair extensions to be beautiful? Have we been hoodwinked by the hair care industry? This goes for all women. Being naïve at times, I was introduced to hair extensions by an European American friend of mine years earlier. She laughed when I told her I thought all the hair on her head was hers! She educated me on the fact white women had been wearing extensions for years and not many have the long hair that we see them wearing.

Back to my new employer and this current situation, I was surprised when she told me that she knew how the chemicals leak through the scalp and ultimately forms on the brain. But with health problems aside, I just wondered how you justified having to take hair from the top center portion of your hair and slick it down to cover those now bare spots near the front and sides. Why is this acceptable, especially when you can administer another routine to care for your own natural hair? I love and respect this woman and she definitely has the same rights to her choices as I do. I am simply asking a question.

Do we or have we come to a place where we hate our ultimate beauty that we would rather be bald than to allow our natural hair to be displayed in all of its magnificence? Without fail each person I know who have allowed their hair to grow in a natural style, dread locs, they are surprised by the longer length and healthier condition of their 'new hair'. This new growth is not damaged by the harsh chemicals. It has been given the freedom to just be what it is and was intended to be, 100% hair.

I have worn my hair in so many styles that I became known for always changing my look. People would be curious to see what style Sandy would be sporting today or at this event. So my comments originate from my gut, my deep level of love for expressing individuality. But even with all the styles, I never abused my hair to the point of losing it; nor causing permanent damage to my hair follicles. Thankfully, I have come to a rationalization and understanding that we are creating our own demons, our self-hatred.

We allow others, anyone outside of ourselves, to define and ultimately determine our beauty. That is giving away your power of choice and freedom. We should understand that the manufacturers of these products must promote their products to demean our natural beauty in some way or another. Otherwise, there is no need for the products they are selling. Have you paid attention to how subtly they tell us we are incomplete without the product on the screen or on the radio or in the magazine ad?

That's called advertising. Most companies would/could not risk you fully appreciating your beauty just as you are. How could they market and sell their products to you? If you knew that just as you are is absolutely beautiful, you would not need to purchase what they are selling. What they do and use are the tricks of the advertising game.

I am not angry with the advertisers nor marketers, not at all. They are simply doing what they are paid to do, advertise and sell the products. What is troubling to me is when women hold their entire image of beauty within that which is created by artificial means. We are created in amazing wonder! We are beautiful creatures! We are Queens! We are BEAUTY IN FULL EXPRESSION!

I had the pleasure of being in the presence of three very beautiful young ladies, an African American, Hispanic and one with Albinism. I could not control myself, I was going on and on about how absolutely beautiful they EACH were with their own unique characteristics. I identified and commented on each of their splendid differences. They just glowed with appreciation that they had been admired. I sincerely meant every word I said to them. They were stunningly beautiful in their natural state.

For me the God of this Universe 'could have made us to ALL look alike'. Yet The Creator was so purposeful in providing separate identity to each of us. Even identical twins are not really identical and have their own unique blueprint of cells, chromosomes and genes.

Do you grant yourself permission to say how much you love and approve of yourself? Do you look into the mirror and fall madly in love with the image you see reflected back at you?

So why is it that we go to all lengths to look alike? Or must wear a certain designer clothing label or shoe label? Now I have been a shoe connoisseur and loved my shoes! But gosh I can't even imagine a working person paying thousands of dollars for a single pair of shoes. That's ludicrous. I can think of so many other things that could be done with that amount of money, like travel and explore this massive universe. Like donate to the homeless and hungry here in America first then to other countries in need of financial help. How about reaching back and helping a family member, an elder or a community center that's struggling to survive financially? Passing some food for thought here, nothing more, and nothing less than that. Simply making an observation. You make your very own choices here. Just a little regression because some of the advertising tactics used merely *'pimps'* us into buying foolishly.

So where does or who gets to define and describe you in terms of your beauty? Do you grant yourself permission to say how much you love and approve of yourself? Do you look into the mirror and fall madly in love with the image you see reflected back at you? Who is saying that we must be paper thin or anorexic to be beautiful? Some crazed men with a fetish for young girls? Only young girls are thin with no body sculpting to emphasize their woman-ness. That whole concept is a bit scary to me. One day I happened to look up at the TV with a new set of eyes and saw for my first time the women that are betrayed as 'models' and beautiful…I mean I really looked closely. They simply reminded me of those children you see on TV that are starving and close to malnutrition!

> *So where does or who gets to define and*
> *describe you in terms of your beauty?*

And we just accept this notion of beauty without the slightest bit of twinge. When I owned a Modeling Company in Los Angeles; Nu Vision Modeling and Entertainment, what I learned was fascinating. The Big, Bold Beautiful Models always strutted with no pretense, no shame, and no guilt. I was captivated by their confidence and insistence on others accepting them just the way they were. They had nothing to prove to anyone. They approved of themselves. And they fiercely approved of themselves, straight no chasers.

The children were not expected to maintain a certain weight or body image to model with Nu Vision Modeling and Entertainment. They were required to maintain acceptable grades in school, get along with others including their parents and they could not be involved with drugs, gangs or become pregnant. Our children were the Ultimate Stars! They shined bright enough for the whole world to catch a glimpse of them as they strutted on the stages of the major Hotels and Convention Centers in Los Angeles. The models excelled not at being thin enough to see through, but rather because they were being trained to handle life after they left the studio. They received invaluable training, information and counseling to carry them through the tough spots of life. They learned and as was required of them, they passed the knowledge on to others.

They learned to love themselves at whatever stage of life they were in. And however their body reflected that image, we concentrated on the wellness of it and not the thinness of it. Who came up with the notion that thin is beautiful anyway? I remember Twiggy from the 1960's. Everyone gasped when she was introduced to the public! I do not believe the term anorexia was created until after Twiggy made an entrance to the stage. When we watch a program that depicts hungry, starving children they are usually extremely thin. So does that not mean that thin represents illness? I'm just saying, we had better begin thinking for our self and refuse to listen to what others are telling us. Perhaps refuse to listen is too harsh, yet we should question what we are accepting as blind-faith truth. We do have an opportunity in this life to think for ourselves. You are the master of your fate, the captain of your soul

Personally, I can climb up mountains and through car windows as others watch in amazement. I keep going when I have agreed to do a task. I seek the best in life and in others. What I get in return is the best life has to offer. I am the only one who gets to set my limits on life and living. And when this physical life is over, may my legacy be one of possibilities and options. For all who really know me, may they be blessed to never consider living within the confines of 'the box' as sufficient evidence of having lived life. The box is merely an imaginary device to control the vision and possibilities that are available to each of us. The box is a coffin!

In my eyes, we are each Beautiful Expressions of Love by The Creator. What do you see in your mirror?

I see your innate beauty glowing fully. I see the wonder in your eyes. I see perfection of a life that was sculpted by the God of all living creatures. I see YOU in all your infinite possibilities. I see you now looking to see if you can see the same thing in your mirror. Your mirror is your gift. Learn to look with eyes of complete acceptance and amazement. Learn to look closer to find the one person who loves you beyond all situations and conditions. Learn to look with LOVE at you, my friend.

You are a miracle, a one of a kind unrepeatable masterpiece! Within you is all the beauty that life has to offer. You are crafted to perfection! Your image is unmistakably divine. Enjoy your life.

What do you see when you look in your mirror?

Beauty is in the eye of the beholder.....Are you looking at BEAUTY?

Do you LOVE who you are??

My many faces.....

Have included braids as a child and adult. As a child I had no choice. As an adult I enjoyed the flexibility of the braids. They were usually accomplished with the aide of hair extensions/purchased hair. The styles were endless, only limited by the hair stylists' imagination. I served as a hair model for several stylists, especially while residing in Los Angeles.

Many years saw me sporting a relaxed or chemically straigthened hair-do! As a small child I could barely wait until I was old enough to get my hair 'permed'. That was a sign of growing up. When you were allowed to go from 'hot comb' to a perm was a sign of maturity. Sidenote: the use of a 'hot comb' by most everyone resulted in burned ears, neck or back of knuckles/hand/fingers! At least for me that was my reality. Always a burned something!! Great memories.

I had the courage to wear my hair naturally in an afro style both as a teenager and as an adult. Both times were an

indication of my preference. To wear your hair naturally meant there were no chemicals applied to the hair or scalp. Wash/shampoo, condition apply some oil/moisturizer maybe braid and that was it. The braiding allowed the hair to be lengthened by loosening some of the natural curl to the hair. I absolutley adored myself when I wore my hair in a natural afro style. I was bold and brave. I felt it. I lived it.

I wore my hair in Dreadlocs twice. The first time I allowed my hair to grow for aboout seven years. My hair grew down to my waistline. Never had I ever been able to grow my hair that long. My second round of growing Dreadlocs only lasted about three years but still my hair had grown down past my shoulders. I firmly believe that given a chance to grow without chemicals, the hair will do what it does best – grow! I have witnessed this time and again. Hair left to its natural ways will do what it does best. The chemicals causes imbalances and confusion to the hair follicles. The hair becomes distressed and unable to grow.

And now, turning 65 in 2015 I have yet another show of fierce independence. Currently I wear a 'bald head'. It expresses a liberation for me. A liberation from all of the hype of wearing additional hair, extensions/weaves. Looking around, all I see is women of all nationalities wearing long tresses. Its not thiers other than they have purchased it. And some of the prices are ridiculous. But that's another story all by itself. Being bald affords me yet another way to express my creativity and individualism. Recently a small child laughed when he saw me and my bald head. The mother chastised him and told him that his actions were rude and unkind. His reply was 'Why mommy? She looks very pretty!' Once my admirer learns my style is not the result of a health issue they allow themselves to appreciate my boldness and freedom. I have many women who will openly explain they wish they had the courage to wear such a style. Men find it sexy and appealing.

One of my male friends in particular had not commited to his approval when we attended an event together. He is a people watcher and so this night was very special to him. He secretly wanted to witness how people responded to my baldness. He was amazed. He told me he watched as women appeared to envy my style. He overheard a few of them commenting on my gorgeousness, his words not mine!

I have a few men that say they just want to kiss my bald head! And one who always has to rub my head whenever he sees me. On the days that I don't shave and have stubbs I tell him not to rub today! We both laugh and he will usually say, "Oh so you did not shave today?!"

Some in my immediate family don't quite get it or me! I feel some will not tell me exactly what they think. Others say, "Leave it to Sandy to always surprise us with her latest looks!" Probably my fondest response was from my great-niece Nyala who wanted to know if I had the 'cancerous'. She was terrified to ask me directly so she prompted her Aunt, Tia Tifah, my niece to ask me. But before she turned to ask me she assured Nyala that was the reason why she and her siblings loved to hang out with Aunt Sandy, she always did unusual things especially wearing her hair in different styles!

And I am still growing and changing!

LEARNING VALUE IN OUR STORY

Oftentimes the only obstacle blocking us from receiving of the vast abundance God has for us is accepting our 'value and worth.' By Rev. Sandy Rodgers

Many have been led to deny their story; by hearing 'keep your business to yourself', 'don't put our or your business in the streets', or similar phrases. Maybe we discounted our feelings because we heard, 'things aren't that bad.'

We hear powerful and amazing religious sermons, attend top-rated seminars and yet somehow we feel things just are not changing in our life. We remain in the same spot, longer than we want.

It's time to tell our story, to validate our worthiness and open ourselves to receive ALL that God has – just for US! Once we own our feelings, whatever they are now or have been in the past, we receive grace. The first step is own up to our feelings. Grace is there waiting for us.

When we know we are whole, complete and healthy children of God, we can tell our story proudly. We know that God has brought us <u>through</u> to this moment to serve as a blessing to ourselves and others. Our trials, tribulations and subsequent victories prepared us for who we are today. The past is gone, Thanks God.

As we each share our story healing has taken place in wondrous ways.

Accepting our true nature of 'goodness', we can fully receive and apply the prosperity lessons we are learning. We say 'Yes' to God and to ourselves. Go ahead and give yourself liberty to tell your story. We can write it out. We can share within a safe environment, for example a loving support group or trusted friend. We may even find while sharing that our story is the same as another. We are each a part of the 'One Family of God.'

Doing this exercise during my weekly sessions within the HIV/AIDS community has brought new life springing forth from these individuals. They had accepted they were no good and good for nothing. As we each share our story healing takes place in wondrous ways. The group is extremely supportive and encourages each other to tell the whole story. We intentionally feel the Pains!

We share about drug use and abuse. We tell about our childhood horrors of being molested or raped. We share from a place of safety knowing the others will still embrace us with unconditional love. We tell of that incident that removed, damaged or destroyed our innocence.

We trust and know that our past is just that, over and done with… it has passed. The past is something we cannot change. We then place total forgiveness around the situation and persons involved, including and most importantly ourselves.

We proceed to wrap the situation and people in absolute love. Lives are changing. New life is ever present and springing forth daily. The individuals are currently doing things that they thought were impossible. They are going back to school to learn a new trade, computer skills; careers in the medical field among others. Moving out from the shelters into their own homes is another result. New thoughts equal new realities which equal freedom.

This is happening because they have been freed from the shackles of their past. They have allowed a new thought to be entertained in their thinking, memory and hearts. Our stories are real and worthy to be told. We are worthy and deserve to live a full life void of unforgiveness and bitterness. It is possible to release, forgive and love any and all unpleasant situations from your past. It is now time to live life fully in harmony and joy. The first step is our willingness to release and let it go.

Whatever is holding you back from fully experiencing life, remember it, forgive it and then love it! This is the way to a wonderful life experience here on earth. Your story is whatever you say it is, it does not have to be true for anyone other than yourself. So tell it. Celebrate your victory over the past. Honor exactly where you are this very day and LIVE!

Watch miracles unfold as you lovingly embrace your awesome, wonderful self.

> *"I accept the Essence of my human function.*
> *I joyfully Display My Full Human*
> *Magnificence." Rev. Sandy Rodgers*

LOVING IS...

Copyright 2011 © Sandy Rodgers

Full Acceptance

Nothing to change or alter

Listening without judgments

not wanting to Fix

or control.

Being a friend

through all the

challenges of life.

Providing a Peaceful Environment.

STAGE 2

Sitting

SITTING

"...I relinquish everything and SIT!!!"

"Oh that's stupid!!!" 'You better get up and do something.' The number of times I have said this to myself is beyond counting. Even while meditating (ha ha) the thought would come 'You don't have time to be sitting still. Girl you dun lost your ever-loving mind!' But SIT – I had to.

Recently I was reminded of the Faith of our animals. A friend was describing his scenery of squirrels jumping from here to there, branch to branch. As he observed he said, "It amazes me how they jump on the smallest branch and keep going." "WOW" was my response. We humans are always looking for a tree trunk before we take the first step or move in another direction. The animals are some of our best teachers of life and trust.

The deeper the opportunity, the longer I SIT!

Now, whenever I consider the walls to be collapsing all around and over me - I relinquish everything and SIT! The length of time varies from a few moments to days to weeks and even months. The deeper the opportunity, the longer I SIT!

As for me, a person professionally trained and conditioned by corporations on goal setting, I am firmly associated with daily to-do, no make that hourly to-do lists. Well it ain't been easy. I prided myself on accomplishments that were measured by the many to-do lists. I learned numerous methodologies to track my successes. Maybe the one I enjoyed the most involved color coding by priority or upon completion. This was a different way of tracking my time and it was very colorful and I believe that is what made me like it so much. Each color signified the importance of the chore/task. For instance, red symbolized highest priority, blue next highest and so on.

And some times I play games on the computer.

There is nothing wrong with to-do lists; I used them for years with great achievement of some very worthy goals. Just in case the lists no longer excite nor ignite nor invigorate you, you are perhaps beyond this task. I still use them occasionally.

Currently, I sit and become still. Sometimes I soak in a salt bath, other times I sit on the floor or lay in the bed. And some times I play games on the computer. This may sound strange or foolish to you. Well here is why it works for me. As I play games on the computer and with me being such a competitive player, I get completely caught up in the game. My mind cannot stray away to my opportunities, worries or concerns. My mind is totally involved in winning the game on the computer. So even if it looks like I'm wasting time, which is what I told myself repeatedly, I am not. I am actually more focused and my mind has been given an opportunity to rest from its constant thought processes. I had a friend to tell me recently that he is glad he is not me because it appeared that my mind was always involved in some heavy thinking. That my mind was always on high-alert! I laughed because he is right and that is the reason the computer is so therapeutic for me. The most profound challenges I faced were solved during one of these computer games. The right action to take to solve a situation or the right person to contact became the perfect resource that appeared during one of my games. Some very silly thoughts (my analogy – of course) proved to be extremely important and beneficial to the current situations/opportunities in my life.

Sitting – oh the fear of not 'doing' some thing; something. Prior to learning the value in sitting, I experienced anxiety attacks, nervous skin rashes and outbreaks, restlessness and fear. Fear reared its head and begged me to get up and 'do' something. It did not matter what activity I engaged in just 'do' something! Sitting proves itself over and over again in my life and in the lives of many of my friends who can and will sit with a challenge in their life. Sitting is being at Peace with life and you. Sitting is allowing grace into your existence.

Sitting allows your body and mind to relax and recuperate. We are not required to be a body that is always 'in motion'. We can stop periodically and just sit; to smell the roses; to observe nature; or to be at Peace!

By waiting it out, the negative emotions subsided and eventually left me. I trust the Power of the stillness, the blessings of stopping activity and being still while I SIT!

I imagine Maya Angelou would probably say, **A bird sings because it has a song, and not for any other reason. In the sitting Beloved, you may find <u>your</u> song!**

DIVINE DETOUR

"...proceed on the new opened path."

Have you ever had your vision set on one goal, only to arrive somewhere else or that certain destination is not available to you?

I have learned to call those times, Divine Detours! It seems I always end at a place for greater understanding and higher learning. Situations and people that provide me with a greater opportunity to experience life are always at the detour! Certainly there are more lessons in the blessings.

So next time you aim for a particular goal or are maneuvering to a certain destination and it appears difficult to reach – Look for the lessons that life has for you. Receive the opulent unexpected blessings!

God is truly blessing you, even though it may not look the way you envisioned it.

Give THANKS and proceed on the new opened path (and have some FUN).

POSITIVE THOUGHTS

"Wherever I go – I must be there!"
"Leadership is pure influence."
"All Leaders are readers."
"Live where Lives are changing."
"Build relationships, listening is always twice as important."
"Be OUTSTANDING all the time!"
"Pull the future into the present, like using a fishing pole."
"Excuses do not exist in the Big League."
"My Choice = Tidal Wave or little production."
"Keep Commitment to My Commitment!!!"
"I LIVE MY COMMITMENT."
"I will fail my way to success."
"Anger is the wind that blows out the flame of success."
"Ask for help. Don't stop asking til I get it."
"No test – No testimony!"
"Dreams carry you through the nightmares of the day!"
"GREATNESS IS WITHIN!"
"The world is waiting for my story!"
"Looking for everyone who knows they deserve more than what they have!"
"ELEVATE MYSELF AS YOU ELEVATE YOURSELF!"

HOW TO NOURISH YOU EVERYDAY

Releasing Rituals:

- Be still and relax
- Take small mini-vacations throughout the day
- Make more hours in your day that can free you for some "me-time"
- Love yourself – 'Do Unto Yourself as you would do for others'
- Take Care of yourself
- Set priorities with your time
- Prepare your surroundings to assist you in relaxation, positive energy generation and successful completion of your objectives.
- Meditate
- Eat healthy nutritious foods, real food.
- Get some sunshine.
- Breathe. Exhale. Inhale.
- Smile! Have FUN!
- Show Gratitude, Appreciation, Be Thankful.

Caregivers:

As America faces an "aging population" challenge, more and more people are being cast into the roles of "Caregivers" to an aging parent, spouse or friend. Coupled with caring for their own households they are the "invisible and endangered components" in today's health care support system. Caregivers are a special breed of humans who willfully compromise and offer their lifestyle over to care for someone close to them, a loved one.

Statistics prove that many caregivers burn out physically and emotionally before the ones they are caring for. Due to the stress and limited attention to their own needs, they themselves can become incapacitated, no longer able to care for those who depend on them. This is not done for the caregiver to be known as a martyr, but rather because the caregiver truly wants to be of the greatest benefit to those they are caring for. Without proper awareness or training the burnout can happen quickly and without notice.

Wholistic programs designed to provide the caregiver with coping mechanisms, physical and mental exercises to maintain their own health, are well worth investigating. Caregivers require de-stressing and health enhancing techniques that they can utilize to bring their bodies into harmony and balance. Inclusion of daily mini-breaks, breathers can aide in the detoxing of the emotions and regeneration of the mental body. Fresh air circulating inside the body temple reduces negative ions.

Sessions can/may include meditation, exercise, breathing techniques, Reiki treatments, Stress Control, yoga, time saving suggestions, and Feng Shui. An atmosphere which supports general sharing of information where they are allowed and encouraged to tell their story in a loving, supportive and compassionate atmosphere, can help them in their healing. This is termed "debriefing", "laying your burdens down" or "leaving it at the altar". Tell it and release that energy to make space for your rest and rejuvenation. Caregivers are to be applauded for their sacrifices. Many do not want the applause because their motivation is to be of service and for no other reason. The care of the loved one is of the utmost importance and nothing more.

However even with the most well-intentioned plan a personal program can be beneficial. The program you choose should provide each caregiver with the techniques they can use to take mini-mental breaks or mini-vacations during their busy day, thus enabling them to be rested, relaxed, revitalized and rejuvenated.

If a program does not exist in your area, perhaps you can design and implement one to be of service to those who are serving in the roles of caregivers. Caregivers are a special group of people!

STAGE 3

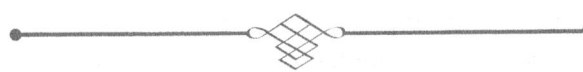

Remembering

REMEMBERING OUR BEAUTY IN TOUGH TIMES

"Then I saw their nurturing spirit, their gentleness, the mother's care and the givers of unconditional love."

Why Remember ?

Tough times are described differently for each individual. Tough times may seem to last forever or for just a fleeting moment. Tough times may mean the loss of a loved one-through death, divorce, relocation, or break-up. Tough times can be unemployment, being single, raising children alone, or suffering the pangs of becoming mature. Tough times can be rape, incest, or molestation. Tough times can be rejection or abandonment of one or both parents. Tough times may be watching your grown children travel their path, a path so different from the one you envisioned as you labored to give birth and watched them grow up. Tough times may be having an abortion, miscarriage or not being able to have children. Tough times can be hanging onto a relationship long after the loving has stopped. Tough times can simply be NOT KNOWING YOU ARE A CHILD OF GOD. Tough times are whatever you decide they are.

<u>Stop here and breathe. Exhale slowly. Okay take one more deep breath and slowly blow the air out.</u>

Tough times are only temporary, particularly when we remember to honor our strength and beauty. These two attributes dwell in each of us. For some of us the weeding process may take longer than others. Due largely to the very deep and overgrown roots that are attached to the weeds. As all gardeners know, the complete and thorough removal of unwanted growth (weeds) must be accomplished before realizing the beauty in a splendid garden.

> *"I saw women who were experiencing
> tough times and asked for help."*

Sisters, friend at some point in our lives we have all had tough times! The delicate and glorious rose is atop a branch composed of thorns, but the thorns do not and should not conceal us. The thorns represent those times we have grown through to reach our true, innate beauty. The thorns serve as a protection to the beautiful flower. The thorns stop danger from happening. "A rose by any other name would smell just as sweet." It is time to rediscover and reveal our beautiful petals. Sisters we have a powerful responsibility to the balance of creation. Made in HIS/HER likeness, GOD created man and woman. I describe the latter as:

Womb
Of
Mankind
And
Nature

I have chosen one of the world's most beloved flowers: the Rose. It is often presented as a gesture of love and kindness. The image is strong, the smell is sweet and the color is brilliant. It is a representation of woman. I share with you the power of the Rose which captivates the mind, body and spirit while fulfilling its purpose. Simply put, woman, you are the Rose and the Rose Garden becomes your life:

R Radiating
O Our
S Spiritual
E Essence

The Rose must be carefully tended to produce the desired outcome. It requires love and gives love, just like the woman whose love is deeply planted in the garden of creation. Our Heavenly Father created man and woman in His likeness. I believe this empowers us to live our lives as a blessing to others and ourselves with the tenderness of all love.

One evening I approached the podium to deliver an inspirational talk to a group of women and their children living in a battered women's shelter in Atlanta Georgia. I looked deep into the eyes of these beautiful women, down to the depths of their souls. I felt the sorrow in their tearful eyes, their misguided trust, their sense of hopelessness and loneliness. Then I saw their nurturing spirit, their gentleness, the mother's care and the givers of unconditional love. I saw Roses in a garden that needed to be tended. I saw women who were experiencing tough times and asked for help.

Our goal is to become whole and focus on a healthier and happier mind, body and spiritual awareness. Do you want a garden of love, joy, peace, and harmony? All you need is faith the size of a mustard seed.

So my mission is to help rewrite our story – HER STORY.

"Sisters our strength is our softness."

To allow every woman to define for herself – who she is. To allow women to burst out of the womb of oppression (harshness, competing with men, being a hoochie mama, etc.) and create for herself a new womb of endless opportunity!

We must tend to the garden (our lives) and rid ourselves of unwanted weeds. We must no longer allow ourselves to be battered and abused when we feel unlovable (weed). We succumb to drugs (weed) and alcohol (weed) to dull our pains of loneliness and unworthiness (weeds). We use negative self-talk (weed) and make unwise choices (weed). We prostitute our bodies (weed) by allowing obscene visions and words (weed) to describe us. We dress provocatively (weed) to attract the opposite sex. Then, after allowing these weeds to fully overtake our beautiful garden, we wonder how we got into trouble in the first place. We forget, we are the Rose. When we tend to our garden, our spiritual nature reveals the beauty we already possess.

Our very nature is cooperation.

What qualifies me to stand before the Universe speaking on women's issues was not earned in a College or University. What qualifies me is I see myself in every woman I encounter and respond. I honor and respect their awesome presence and listen for HER STORY. Each of us has the ability to respond, to take responsibility to help one another to reach our full potential and desires. I take this responsibility of unconditional love seriously and pray daily for guidance.

Sisters our strength is our softness. When we begin on a journey of healing, or healing has begun, we reach a point of humility. At this point, we are open and receptive to allow others into our lives as a blessing in our quest for a better life. Our very nature is cooperation. In this Spirit, we unite forces, bring harmony, and ensure balance. Our strength is very different from our male counterparts. Our strength is our softness, gentleness, our sweetness.

I am not ashamed of any part of my life

Mothers and Elders we must heal ourselves to return to a state of wholeness. We must accept and acknowledge we are complete, worthy individuals. It is only at this stage that we can role model that confidence to the upcoming generations. That is our job to do.

I remember the deliberate love and compassion of our ancestors who are my inspiration. I humbly ask for their blessings and guidance as we write and rewrite Herstory and tell the truth about History. Their sacrifices and prayers have sung their way into our hearts, but their heartbeats have become fainter as the years pass. We need to embrace their teachings and establish an unyielding trust in the omnipotent, omniscient, omnipresence of God. It's time to be a blessing and honor them with the strength of our heartbeats.

My heart is full with the joyful responsibility to tell the truth of who and Whose we are. We are SO VERY SPECIAL!! Shout it loud and clear from every roof and mountaintop. I stand with a host of believers who know how beautiful we are. First, you have to believe in yourself. (Sing the song Lena Horne).

I am not ashamed of any part of my life, not the excruciatingly painful or the blissfully ignorant periods. Through it all I learned my lessons well. I have a testimony that is definitely real, my real life experiences.

'Seeking The Fullest Manifestation of Myself as a Human Being.' Rev. Sandy Rodgers

NOT THE MIRROR

Are you afraid to look in your mirror because of what someone said to you? Do the harmful words of a cruel comment still play havoc within your spirit? Does your body cringe with the thought of admiring your own body image? Do you fight and insist that the words did not affect you? Does looking at your 'naked' body in a mirror scare the hell out of you?

"Where energy flows…" is a common statement many have used over the years. Simply what this complete declaration means is if your attention is on 'not accepting' a statement, or a negative impact on your life that is where your energy flows. Scientific research has proven that our sub-conscious mind does not differentiate with the words we use. Our mind manifests our thoughts. Simply because you/we use the word 'not' that alone does not change the effect the message has on our reality. So in essence, you are not preventing it but creating more of it. We must change our focus to express what it is we truly desire and want in our life. (We will discuss this more as we move along the path.)

Where you called fat? So now even though you only weigh 100 pounds you feel like you are still overweight. You wear a size 2 and that seems to be too big. Your effort to be an acceptable size is always out of reach for you. Those words of condemnation are constantly in the back of your mind, screaming at you. The words sound so fresh and new. You shiver to remember exactly when this began. All you desire to do is be thin, not called 'fat' in your head/memory. You practice different harmful methods to maintain a skinny pseud. You realize you have held on to these grimacing statements all your life only to find no validity in them now at all. Until you consciously change that insensible image it will ruin your life. Your mirror reflects <u>your</u> thoughts of you! It is all an illusion. You are beautiful. You are worthy.

Did the well-meaning authority figures tell you that you are ugly or no one will ever like you because of the way you look? Each culture has its own set of references to the facial and other features that are intrinsic to that culture. I have heard many of them because I have associated myself with a diverse set of people all my life. As if people can magically change the characteristics of their culture. Yet we have also managed to manipulate the Creator's plan and created the surgical knife to alter whatever feature we find unattractive. This can be a tragic practice to those who are deeply affected by their dislike of their unique features. For it seems they never tire of finding yet another feature to alter.

In some cultures, the young people simply accept what they are being told as the undeniable truth. Many bury the hurtful things said to them due to the cultural norms. Yet these words sting. The statements may have propelled a generation past to some positive movement yet they are now disturbing. Self-hatred or self-sabotage can be the results of such actions from the elders or others in the tribe/community. When we accept less than admirable words to describe who we are, a deep layer of resentment begins to develop at our core. Our heart aches when we do not know we are perfect as we are created. The ignorance goes from one generation to the next as if maintaining some sort of badge of honor. Self-loathing and self-denial are dangerous.

Perhaps some of this language has caused the evidence of violent behavior in people. It may have produced serial killers or child abusers, the wife beaters or the murderers. The language may have led to mental disorders or be evidenced by low grades or non-performance in school by our children. This less than ideal way of communicating one's value is detrimental to the wholeness and vitality of the world community. Perhaps the onslaught of sickness, disease, violence all have their origin in the language of our primary years. Remember our thoughts create our reality.

Children accept this language, this bodily image definition because it is a person of authority that is telling them this. It could have been a parent, a teacher, a member of the church or an older sibling. We think words do not have any power. We are simply repeating what was said to us. But words have an extremely powerful effect on us and the value we see in ourselves. The language can either bless or curse, it cannot do both simultaneously. Are we building up or tearing down? Please pay attention from this point forward to the very words you use to communicate with others, especially our youth.

Words are damaging! Words create images! Words can destroy self-esteem!

So in the end, we hate:

Our nose	**Our way too-long legs**
Our Hips	**Our mouth**
Our flat chest	**Our lips**
Our voluptuous breast	**Our skin tone**
Our squinty eyes	**Our facial features**
Our nappy hair	**Our very uniqueness**
Our too curly hair	**Our distinct characteristics**

We hear young children insisting they are incapable of performing a task even before they attempt to do it for the very first time. Why do these children stop? Children stop short of achieving their greatness, mainly because they are given words of defeat from their authority persons. Children in inner city schools are often misled to believe they are not intelligent enough to consider going to college. Many never explore their genius or consider reaching higher heights. Many simply stop dreaming or never start. The graveyards are filled with unmet dreams and aspirations. Too many stopped short of their fulfilling their contributions to society. I know because I have witnessed it too many times. I have personally heard the stories from those most affected by these statements. Some may actually believe that negative criticism is good to effect a positive outcome. Not sure why the critics feel this way. I am asking for you, the reader, to offer words to uplift and inspire not condemn and belittle.

It then takes a majority of our adult years to counteract the words that were given to us in plentiful supply to thwart our progress in life. All of these proclamations stunt our ability to see ourselves as we really are. We are indeed each a worthy, unrepeatable miracle in human expression! We are sufficient unto our self. We are more than enough. Yet not many will tell us how powerful we really are. Few will give us permission to boast of our beauty or intelligence.

Many of us succumb to lowered and bowed heads, unable to sincerely accept genuine compliments. When compliments are received we usually deflect the positive energy by minimizing the statement or by pretending we did not hear the words. At some point in our lives, we are probably each guilty of not being able to comfortably accept a compliment.

And so it is, as we glance into the mirror of our lives, what is it that is being reflected back to you? Is it Joy, Peace, Happiness or Harmony? Is it Love, Beauty, Worthiness? Are you at ease with what you perceive in your mirror? Do you dare change it? Yes, of course if that is your choice. What are your thoughts right now? Do you dare risk changing your thoughts about you? Can this be that simple? Can you learn to accept you just as you are?

You are worthy of all the best life has to offer! You are perfect exactly how you are presently! You are beautiful in and out! You are amazing! You are whole and complete all by yourself! LOVE created YOU! You are a miracle! You are Life! You are LOVE! You are more than enough!

These are the words I tell myself as I look into my personal mirror daily. Perhaps I did not hear them as much as I needed as I was growing up but that's okay. I give myself permission to say these words today and mean them wholeheartedly! I am my best supporter. Because guess what... I can only depend on me for what I need in my life. My inner child knows she is loved beyond measure and that every little part of her is so lovely. I nurture the small child that never received the compliments and adoration. My small inner child knows that she is loved and beautiful. She knows she is acceptable just as she is, period.

In this earthly experience, I am granted inalienable rights to the quest of life, liberty and the pursuit of happiness. I do not allow others to take what is rightfully mine away from me. So therefore I grant no one the right to describe, set my beauty standards nor judge me. I recognize Whose I Am, that of The Creator. The Master of Life. The Most High Energy. The Universe. Love!

I proudly look into my mirror, notwithstanding what I was told the majority of my younger life. I forgive myself for believing it; I forgive whoever said those words to me. It is no longer valid in my life or thoughts. I am a bold and bodacious person, created in a Love so strong that no-thing nor no-one can disturb the belief I hold about me. I look in my mirror with the pride of understanding and acceptance.

Every aspect of who I am is now accepted as a beautiful expression of ME! I love the body temple that houses my spirit. I love the shape of my body. I love the texture of my hair. I love my facial features. I adore what I see in my mirror. My nose is the perfect size. My lips and hips are beautiful. My eyes seem to sparkle. I AM the most wonderful person I know.

This practice is as easy or difficult as you declare it to be. Will you give yourself permission to think a new thought and say only positive words about you? Can you eliminate the negative phrases that you have been silently repeating to yourself for years? Yes it will take some diligent effort on your part. Remember, all new habits require effort, repetition and concentration, this is no different.

Let us crack and dismantle the mirror that has kept us feeling inferior and incapable. Let us toss the mirror of ugly anything out once and for good. We accept beauty in all things, especially within our self. As in the movie, The Help tell your little inner child… *'you is smart, you is kind, you is important!'*

Listen and hear the words of your new mirror. Remember the mirror never lies. Also remember the mirror merely reflects your thoughts!

In Marianne Williamson's Award Winning book ***A Return To Love,*** she offers us her ***Deepest Fear*** piece, which gives these exquisite words to contemplate:

> *Our deepest fear is not that we are inadequate.*
> *Our deepest fear is that we are*
> *powerful beyond measure.*
> *It is our light, not our darkness that most frightens us.*
> *We ask ourselves, Who am I to be brilliant,*
> *gorgeous, talented, fabulous?*
> *Actually, who are you **not** to be?*
> *You are a child of God.*
> *Your playing small does not serve the world.*

> *There is nothing enlightened about shrinking so
> that other people won't feel insecure around you.
> We are all meant to shine, as children do.
> We were born to make manifest the
> glory of God that is within us.
> It's not just in some of us; it's in everyone.
> And as we let our own light shine, we unconsciously
> give other people permission to do the same.
> As we are liberated from our own fear, our
> presence automatically liberates others.*

Are you beginning to see that there does exist a reasonable amount of truth to the statement, **you are more than enough?** There are examples all around us to remind us of our imbedded beauty and talents. We just have a tendency to dismiss them because we have too much nonsensical conversations going on inside our heads. The battles are between what we were told as children and what we now choose to believe. We can stop the battle by insisting we listen only to **our** truth.

That truth is we are intelligent, competent, beautiful individuals. The truth is: the advice we were given and received as children, was sometimes given by wounded people who did not know any better or they thought the advice they gave would propel you to much higher dimensions. In any case, you can change your belief systems if you choose to. When you decide a better existence and legacy is your forte **you will change.** Does the words or memory help or harm you in today's world? If the memory causes negative feelings you do not need to continue to carry them around with you nor believe them any longer.

We are each so special. That is the most important concept we can individually learn about who we are. No one is above or below you, unless you allow them to be. You are such a unique being that there is none other just like you. You alone have the blueprint and fingerprints that make up you! No other living being has the same qualities as you. Even identical twins have separate identities. No two humans are exactly the same. How incredible is that? How miraculous is your life when looking upon it and viewing it from this perspective? There are billions perhaps trillions of people upon the face of this planet and beyond. Can you just for a moment consider the awesome fact that none other have the same identifying qualities as you?? That is simply incredulous to me. It is hard to phantom such a concept. What....only one ME?! Come on now, you may have never thought of life in these terms. But YOU my friend are so unique and special. None like you in this entire Galaxy! WOW

I applaud you in all your wondrous ways. There have been and remains many forces that could not benefit from you truly knowing your self-worth. These entities went about the business of programming your thoughts to accept and believe you were less than others. You were taught you required certain products or classes to be an acceptable human. This was all done through the media; television, magazines, music and sometimes even our educational system and religious organizations.

We are created in pure Love. It is Love that you see reflected back at you in your mirror. You are LOVE, through and through.

I urge you to look lovingly in your mirror and witness for perhaps your first time, a wondrous, strikingly beautiful person. You are masculine. You are feminine. You are LOVE!

MY LIBERATION

I use to be an angry Black Woman
Disguised in beautiful clothes and worldly success,
Now I am Joyous and Free
Yes, this is the Brand New Me!
I wore a bright smile and designer labels,
I always worked hard, giving my best
I enjoyed plenty of public success.
I use to be an angry woman,
Yet I did not know.
Something always seemed to be missing
Money and fulfillment kept at a low.
My life is absolutely perfect,
Just as it should be
Declaring I Am Joyous and Free,
Yes little ol' me.
Did not know I was an angry woman
Until I was totally free.
No one knew,
Not even I,
What shame and guilt
I hid inside.
I have worked diligently to be free
Attended seminars and read the best books
Sat in solitude for countless hours and days
Had to take a look at all my stubborn ways.
Today I am liberated
Right now I am Free.
Take a look at

BEAUTIFUL, AUTHENTIC ME!

STAGE 4

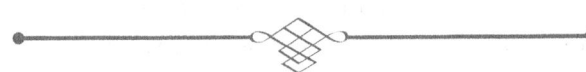

Releasing

'When I choose, I can access The Greater Mind.' Rev. Sandy Rodgers

RELEASING YOUR POWER

"Love others where they are...."

God designed life to be simple. Jesus came to demonstrate to us the ease and joy of human existence. Yet with our intellectual prowess, we have managed to create a very difficult and challenging human existence. We have created countless theories to discount our very core of goodness. Millions of dollars have been spent on or in the quest of self-discovery or self-improvement.

The very language of our formative years, may have taught us to not be great, because in so doing we would become self-centered. As an adult, being self-centered is a good quality, when that centeredness is acknowledging our Christ-consciousness. Self-centeredness only becomes undesirable when we allow the ego to guide and control our actions and words.

When we return to our natural state of pure love, our Christ-self, we simplify our life. The simplicity is living in unconditional love that is not judging people, conditions or situations. When we love completely, we live in a state of total acceptance and full forgiveness. In accepting and forgiving we discover our power, an awesome power that shines brightly through us to illumine our path and makes our way easy to see and understand.

> *The simplicity is living in unconditional love that is not judging people, conditions or situations.*

To release your power, choose to live in the Light and Love of your Christ-consciousness. As you release all held judgments and begin to forgive, miracles will unfold in your life. Life for you will become new. The newness is in seeing everything from a higher consciousness. This action is very liberating and allows the goodness of God to penetrate the very core of your being. As you begin to love unconditionally, you will notice that the act of judging has caused havoc for you. Havoc disguised as physical ailments or unhappy relationships, medical disharmony or dis-eases.

Love is purifying, cleansing the blockages of unforgiveness and judgment.

There is power and new life in Love. Colossians 3:10 states, "You are living a brand new life that is continually learning more and more of what is right, and trying constantly to be more and more like Christ who created this new life within you." (The Living Bible translation). Love is purifying, cleansing the blockages of unforgiveness and judgment. Colossians 3:14, "Most of all, let love guide your life, for then the whole church will stay together in perfect harmony." This also applies to your other relationships as well; in your family, with your friends, on the job and all other encounters. The power you will receive is abundantly rich with blessings of all kinds.

Learn to love. Begin by embracing the uniqueness and diversity in all people. Allow people to express themselves without your judgment. Honor your neighbor with respect. Be a helpmate to those requiring a helping hand or encouraging word. Do not destroy another with negative words or thoughts. Love others where they are. Love yourself unconditionally. Loving is healing in action. This is truly your power and it is enthusiastic and energizing.

Your power of Love is waiting to be released!

Love is purifying, cleansing the blockages of unforgiveness and judgment.

HONOR SELF

It is so extremely important to pause and understand it is your responsibility to honor and care for you, especially in times of celebrating life events which can be both exciting and stressful at the same time.

Your first assignment is to take care of YOU!
Fill your cup first, then and only then from your overflowing resources may you fill someone's cup.

Events that we celebrate such as births, graduations, baptisms, weddings, birthdays, anniversaries, family reunions and other milestones can be happy occasions. And they can be stressful because it is the time when families gather together and celebrate various traditions. Most events are festive, wonderfully decorated and perfect causes to honor. So we go about decorating the house, the yard, the tree, and whatever else we deem appropriate. We shop endlessly for the perfect gift to match the requested item(s) or worry if we are purchasing the right thing.

We become drained and stressed when not handled properly. When we miss balancing these activities, stress seem to overtake even the most sensible person. Stress can rob you of the very life you are seeking to celebrate. Stress can overtake you and create dis-ease in your being. Stress often reduces our normal sense of wellbeing to a position of 'I'll get to it (balance) in a minute… As soon as I finish this or that.' Yet in the meantime your gauge is steadily going lower and lower, rapidly approaching empty.

To honor self means that regardless to what is happening outside of you; YOU remain the one who is priority. You remember to rest; to eat well; to relax; to have some fun, to breathe and to Love you. Nothing gets done unless and until you take the absolute best care of YOU.

Similar to you being on an airplane where the attendant instructs all to place the oxygen mask on yourself first, in case of an emergency, before attending to others. Your first assignment is to take care of YOU.

After the time you have made sure you are first secured, you can assist others with their need or requirement for some air.

Fill your cup first, then and only then from your overflowing resources may you fill someone's cup. We cannot give from our essential supply and deplete it. Like the oxygen, we must always make sure we are satisfied before attempting to handle another person's concerns.

It is not selfish nor self-serving in a negative fashion. Just think about it, how you can give to someone something that you do not possess. So if you have low energy, lack of rest or are just not taking care of you…. What are going to give another person…Exhaustion; Tiredness; or Grouchiness?

Please gift you first! Love you this day more than anything or anyone else! Glow from the inside out with that knowing you have done the absolute best to HONOR SELF!!!

STAGE 5

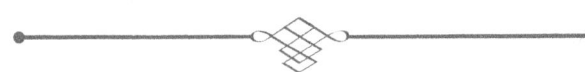

Happiness

RECIPE FOR HAPPINESS

"So fully participate in this day as the sheer gift that it is…"

1. **<u>INTEGRITY</u>**   2 HUGE MEASURES
   (more if needed)

Integrity – What language do you use with yourself when no one else is around to hear what you are saying? What do you tell yourself in the private prism of your mind? Does your light still shine or do you allow it to change, fading away into a nothingness? Are you uplifting with you? Do you speak encouraging words to yourself? Is your tone gentle and reaffirming? Are your words an elixir to your soul? Is there tranquility present?

2. **<u>HARMONY</u>**   SEASON TO TASTE
   (can never have too much)

Harmony – Can you bring harmony to all of your interactions? Will you insist that harmony is ever present with everyone you encounter? Will you think thoughts only of harmony? Does harmonizing thoughts follow you like rays of sunshine? Is the shadow that reflects your Spirit that of harmony? Will you allow harmony to ooze out of every pore of your being? Can you simply sit and think about harmony radiating in the Universe?

4. **<u>JUSTICE</u>**   MAIN SEASONING
   (must be well balanced for a perfect dish)

Justice – Every living being deserves justice! Will you stand up for the small child who is being abused? Will you aide the victims of any type of violence? Can you give comfort to the homeless? Will you speak to the homeless, a simple gesture to respect their being? Can you accept others, especially those that do not look like you? How about those whose behaviors you have deemed unacceptable, strange, or distasteful, is it possible for you to show justice to them? Can you honor justice by judging with reason and balance?

6. **PEACE**	MAJOR INGREDIENT
	(cannot prepare dish without it)

Peace – Peace on Earth and Goodwill to men! How many ways can you demonstrate peace in the world today? In your family? On your job? In your community? Does peace follow you like a second skin? Do you diffuse situations by utilizing the power of peace? Peace has miraculous properties, are you willing to test its power? Will you act on the principle of unbridled peace saturating everything in and on your path?

8. **SERVICE**	LARGE DOSES REQUIRED
	(sweetener)

Service– What is service? Can you find opportunities to serve others? How would you feel when you gave at least 1 day of service monthly to a group or an individual who could truly benefit from your kindness? There is never any act of giving to another in the name of service that is ever too small. To help an elder with yard care or lifting bags at a store or listening with a sincere heart… these are all acts of kindness. Is there just 1 someone you can help today? Or this month? Or consistently?

10. **INTENTIONAL MOVEMENT**	TOP LAYER
	(finishing touch!)

Intentional Movement – For today slow down and move about with an intention to appreciate all that is already freely given to you! Breath. Life. Emotions. Power. Consider what the opposite would be like if it appeared in your reality. Be forever Thankful for ALL things big and small. Smile and tell the world you are thankful to be living on this special day in history. Tomorrow this day will be gone and may even be forgotten, so fully participate in this day as the sheer gift that it is!!

Blessings on the excellent creation!! That's Awesome!! Congratulations....

> *Love is long-suffering and kind; love does not envy; love does not make a vain display of itself, and does not boast. Does not behave itself unseemly, seeks not its own, is not easily provoked, thinks no evil; Rejoices not over iniquity, but rejoices in the truth.* **1 Corinthians 13:4-6, Holy Bible, Lamsa's Aramaic Translation**

WHO WE REALLY ARE – PROUD AND POWERFUL

....

*We cannot get full off crumbs! Emotional
anorexia is not our course in life...*

I actively participated in a Domestic Violence (DV) conference recently. The focus of the DV targeted one specific religious sect. For the purpose of this writing identifying that group is not important. However, the group of women who were represented showcased an extreme of female unworthiness, dishonor and discredit as a human. Females were treated as second-class citizens in their culture. This was difficult to hear initially, the file cases that were used to depict the treatment of these women made the hair on my neck stand up! I received knowledge which enlightened me to this group of individuals who accepted the practices of this religion. And regardless to my judgement or acceptance this was real life for these women. So I chose not to make harsh statements to myself about these women. Not to think awful thoughts about their culture. Rather I chose to learn as much as I could in this event which sought to impart knowledge. In the beginning it was a bit more difficult for the rebel in me not to rise up and be upset. I kept reminding myself that I was there to learn.

I was filled with so much compassion for these females. Because these rituals had been tolerated and accepted for so long, bringing another viewpoint was almost a mute action. Yet the group that hosted this event did just that, they shined the light on the travesties that these women were and are being subjected to even in today's climate. There was power in the summoning of this group of people to uncover and discuss the current issues faced by these women.

When I calmed down and took a closer look at the realities of many other cultures, it may seem that my reactions were a bit much. I graciously accept that to be my truth. Injustice to any group is not respected by me. Injustice to any group is injustice to everyone. I can see myself in every group of people who suffer at the hands of others. Yet history reveals a different view in retrospect.

This inhumane treatment was all done in the name of religion and thus made it acceptable. Yet the atrocities were awful and demeaning to these individuals, the mothers of this culture. How do you enforce rules on anyone that strips them of their spiritual connection with The Creator of all human life? The spiritual connection would demonstrate that they are whole and complete just as the Creator made them. Are the ones inflicting the cruelties afraid of the power of these women? Is the ignorance that makes them feel superior beyond rational thought and understanding? Does the acceptance of these cultural norms allow the offense to be less of an insult against humanity? Those were the questions and concerns going on inside my head.

In this age of history, who could reasonably accept that unimaginable customs are still being followed and adhered to? I pondered this for a long time. I questioned myself on the validity of my statements. I said perhaps it is not my place to pass judgement. But how do I phrase the points that I wanted to make without doing so?

Historically America has always had at least one population that was hated, despised and rallied against. In this setting once again, I learned the lessons of classism, racism, and sexism. My choice is to not add any energy to bigotry of any kind. We are each the same, a human expression of the Most High Creator. Labels and names are merely used to separate individuals. My intention in life is for inclusion of all people, in the activities I engage in. I strongly believe that the many lessons and occasions that have appeared in my life has helped to shape me into understanding the veils that can exist for people. The lessons have come from all avenues in life. I can identify with those labeled as marginal and undeserving, AND those in the penthouses and in Corporate Executive offices.

Females; ladies; women; sisters we must own our Power!! We know a sperm is required, it takes the energy of both male and female to create a new life. We are the chosen ones to carry; birth and nurture new life into this human existence. From this vantage point that makes us extremely strong, resilient, and Powerful. God hand selected us to be the carriers of life!! This has nothing to do with the male energy which is extremely powerful and completely necessary in the balance of life. However, the women must become more understanding of their impact on all humankind. Most men understand their role. And most men would tell you woman, that they would never be able to give birth to a new life. We are heavy-duty warriors in the game of life. We carry and give life to the future of humanity

Where does our 'female' weakness originate? Who told us, we are weak or less than? When did that thinking start? Some men attempt to keep women down because they know women's strength and power!! And furthermore why have we so graciously accepted this put down? Why do we support the same institutions that belittle us? Are we there to offer compassion and help the leaders to return to Love?

Religious textbooks have been written to keep women down. The very language can be understood that women were an after-thought for The Creator! And that the woman is inferior to her male counter-part. The woman disrupted the original creation and so on. And it's funny to me how 'religious' discussions can cause so much conflict, especially for me. It's funny because one would think that as we discuss the Loving Essence that would create all of humanity and all that inhibit the world, that it would be a story of Love and Acceptance. However, while discussing religion there is constantly talk of "sin", "wrong doing", and "consequences".

Calling God a male/man similar to the pictures of Jesus Christ as blonde, and blue-eyed was psychological abuse – sets up women to think themselves as less than or 2nd class. Men have historically used physical violence to control. Women are inherently peace makers, gentle and loving. Men usually initiate 'war', have a "mine is better" attitude, always in a state of competition and comparisons. What if the Energy of all that exists is neither male nor female? What if the Source of all that lives and breathes is Pure Energy or Spirit, without sex or gender? What if man created the necessity to label the gender of The Master Creator? Just something to consider.

America is infamous for wanting others to emulate our actions, even though America was created in cruelty and violence and perpetuated throughout history (his -story). Men normally 'force' an idea and it's usually done with physical actions. Americans think our way is the ***only*** or **best** way! One only need consider the stealing of humans from other Countries or the robbing of the land that was called by another home before it was stolen. Have you ever heard about the Trail of Tears, it is the story of the massive blood shed by Native Indians that inhibited this land and were led in captivity to another less prosperous part of this land that came to be known as The USA? The history can be daunting.

Women or any oppressed group of people cannot get full off of crumbs. It's a form of emotional anorexia, where we allow ourselves to starve within our spirit. Yet our birthright is of royalty and power. Each and every person has the absolute right to dignity and respect… to love and be loved. No one is any more entitled to this freely given gift than another. The Originator of all life gives that to us, not man or laws. All people demand and deserve respect, acceptance, a right to life, liberty, justice and to live in harmony with each other. No threat of terrorism or death should be inflicted on anyone simply because they do not see life exactly as you. We live in a free world and I believe it should be one of Peace.

STAGE 6

My Mirror

MY MIRROR

"None of us can remove the things that life has done to us. They are done before we can realize what's being done, and then make you do things all of your life until these things are constantly coming between you and what you would like to be.
And in that way you seem to lose yourself forever!"

~~~~~~~

When I look in my mirror who do I see? Is it the pains from years and situations past or is it hope for a bright future? Is it dread and doom? Is it optimism and revelation? Am I clear about who I am? Do I know what I want? Am I looking with the eyes of Love or fear? Is your vision blocked by the limitations you have placed on the reflection? Are you locked in a prison of hopelessness? What do you see my dear?

Do I get lost in attempting to shrug off old memories in hopes that they will no longer haunt me if I smile wide enough? Where do the memories come from that seem to be everlasting? As soon as I release a thought another one emerges, as if it is just waiting for me to think it's all under control. These thoughts can consume me with worry and doubt. Thoughts that keep me wide awake all night with insomnia. Thoughts of self-hate plague me....

Is it even possible for me to see a beautiful person in the mirror? What about the things from my past, won't someone remember and remind me? Hell won't I remind myself? After all my biggest fear is facing the mirror of my own life. Wearing a mask has worked for me. Yet now the mask is suffocating me. I feel life is being drained from me without my permission. Stop! I want to live! I am tired of being tired, of not trusting the real me. Somewhere deep down inside is a voice that tells me I am so much more than what I have been saying to myself. Deep inside is the voice of wisdom that will not allow me to suffer any longer. Deep down inside of me is the Spirit that surpasses all human knowledge. This Spirit urges me to be ME, just to BE!

Sometimes I feel like I'm okay and silently hope I can make it through the entire day with only repeating positive affirmations to myself. But as soon as I awaken from the dream I realize that it was just a dream. I want this reality to be real for me throughout the waking hours of my life. I trust I am whole and complete. I trust I was created in absolute, unconditional Love. Yes me, that's my heritage. LOVE!

What and who do I see when I peak in the mirror in front of me? What about all the mistakes I made and my elders telling me 'You won't amount to a hill of beans'? They did tell me those things for my own good, right? Or the teachers that insisted I act like everyone else, can't they see I am my own person? I am unique and want to display that. Yet conformity is the rule of the school. "No, no that is not right. Why can't you be like everyone else?"

Oh that I may see a bright glowing face in the mirror, a face that weathered the storms and emerged unscathed by it all. But is this just wishing and hoping for too much again? I tried to do this before and it had not worked because after all I am a 'good for nothing, no good' person. That's what the Preacher said one day at Church. The Preacher wouldn't lie, right? The Preacher knows all about right and wrong, good and bad. So I must be bad and no good, if the Preacher says it then it is the truth. God knows the Preacher only tells the truth.

Then I looked at the television and saw that I was betrayed as a misfit ...an unruly individual. Well I am sure the movie moguls know who I am, surely they have done extensive research to be able to make these films and documentaries. No, no it's not make-believe, it is the truth of my being up on the big wide mega-screen. There it's been confirmed my life is a waste of human energy. I do not look like the famous, worthy folks on the screen. They all seem to look the same, have the same features. So where did I come from? Was God mad and upset like they said and created a lessor class of people to be the servants of the others? Of course, the movie engineers would certainly not lie about life and then ask us to pay to see their lies, right?

Well what about the folks in my hometown, the elders of the community surely they are wise old persons and would not lie to a child. They have told me all sorts of things that sounded real to me as I was growing up. Go to school, get good grades, obey all the rules and your life will be fine.

Then you will get married, have children and life will be even better. Oh how excited to venture out into life and receive all of the good things I was told I would have, if I followed all the rules. I did that but what happened? Where is my golden life that they promised I would have? I followed all the rules. Had some bumps along the road but still I managed to complete all the tasks assigned to me. Even excelled in most. No one could beat me up more than I did when I missed being number 1 in any undertaking. I was warned to be the best or lose the game. I never wanted to lose a game not even one!

When I look deep into my mirror, do I see unmet dreams or false hopes? Do I still harbor ill feelings for all the bogus things told me? When I look in my mirror, what and who do I see? Am I at peace with the reflection starring back at me? What say you, mirror? Is what I am looking at an illusion? Could it possibly be that I am more or at least different from what I have thought?

I choose this very day to see ME as never before. I see beauty. I see possibility. I see potential. I see power. I see Love. I see peace. I see a powerhouse capable of manifesting and living in a world of unseen possibilities! I see trust and faith and power and worthiness! I see a whole and complete person! I see a Blessed person, filled with admiration and gratitude!

I see what I have been missing, attempting to live someone else's version of my life. My life is good and I am even better than that. I am harmony. I am justice. I am hope. I am wonderful. I am amazing.

The reflection in the mirror is of a marvelous person who has lived a very good life, learning the necessary lessons along the journey. There are no accidents. I got the lessons I needed to live a bountiful life. My journey has been a good one. Sometimes it has been tough yet good just the same. And I must confess, it has had many ups and downs. Yet it is okay, that is what life is all about. We get to learn in the down times, in the valley experiences are real life stories. Life cannot all be up all the time. That would make life so extremely boring.

Whoever said life would be easy was merely attempting not to frighten me. My life has been extremely colorful and the blessings and lessons have been many. Right now I would not change anything, not one little bit of my rich history. It was all the colors of my past that have made me into this wondrous person I am today! I am grateful.

As I strut to the mirror; My head is held high. My stride is perfect and straight. It is ME in the mirror. Proud. Strong. Lively. Joyous. Interdependent. Loving. Free.

I have a choice of how I choose to remember my yesterday. No more sorrow or regrets. No more should've, could've or would've. No self-pity. No condemnation of me allowed.

My mirror is radiant and full of life! The vision I see is me. I am radiant and full of life. I trust the process of life to be what it is. I can, I will and do finally release all of the garbage I have carried with me for years. All of the crap is forever gone back into a nothingness of smoke. Swish it's gone!! Bye Bye.

What an incredible feeling to know I have the power to make meaningful choices in my life that are reflected back at me in MY MIRROR! Oh happy day.... I am Thankful.

STAGE 7

Masculine

THE MAN IN THE MIRROR

This song made famous by the incomparable Michael Jackson has deep implications. Michael's lyrics asked the listener to start with the person in the mirror to make the change that they wanted….

If You Wanna Make The World
A Better Place
Take A Look At Yourself, And
Then Make A Change

How can you make a change without acknowledging what you see in your mirror? Men are not typically expected to spend time gazing into a mirror. Some feel it is a little too girly. Yet we each as a person have access to a mirror, even if only in passing. The mirror is our reflection.

Most men naturally, or not, assume this stance of masculinity that tells them and the world 'I'm STRONG. I don't cry. I have no fears.' Do not expect me to care about anything, because I will not and cannot. This is just one of the misnomers of life. But it helps to erect a false selfhood for men. The misunderstanding of the word macho places a heavy burden on the masculine soul. Each human alive has the same capacity of emotions. Each of us have ups and downs, highs and lows, good times and not so good times. We each hurt and experience pain. We can be happy or not. The emotions are not restricted to females but we sometimes behave as if that is true.

Yet the majority of men I have known present a more humane appearance than what is projected through various media outlets. I know thousands of men from all walks of life. Many of whom I write about in my premiere book, *'All My Men'*. I tell of men who represent all of mankind from the man living on the streets to the Executive in the high rise office building, Presidents and CEO's of large corporations. Some 500 men are honored in this book

When listened to, men have volumes to share. They wait, hoping that along their path will be a single soul interested enough to listen, truly listen to what they have to say. And the person must have a non-judgmental ear and heart. No threat of condemnation can be sensed or felt. Honesty is the foundation of the discussion. This is but the beginning of complete acceptance.

As my older brother William Saafir states in my debut book 'All My Men', "Any time a father has to wrestle with his emotions and force himself to hug his own teenage or adult son, something is seriously wrong. While that is bad enough, it is often even more difficult for a father to tell his older son that he loves him, even though he loves him very much. This emotional tug of war causes deep-seated psychological problems for the father and the son. To top it all off, the worst part of this problem is that it has the tendency to repeat itself."

This deep seated psychological problem undermines a person's worth. The damage might very well be done below one's conscious attention. It can hinder a man from looking in the mirror and honoring the image that he sees. Perhaps a question comes to mind for the man, what if male energy is un-lovable or only valuable in brute actions or mentality? What are the influencers that impact a person's internal conversations? Why can't a man love his male children? And this has the tendency to be generational is a curse indeed. Who authored the illusions men are trapped in regarding their emotions? Is there any value in a man disowning his natural instincts?

Another excerpt from 'All My Men'...So much time and negative energy is lost by bashing the Black man and blaming the White man for all the injustices in our society. Both have helped me to learn about life, living, love and the pursuit of happiness. There is no bitterness in my heart or thoughts, just the same unconditional love that has been extended and shared with me. I now understand and fully accept the men that could not demonstrate love perhaps did not know how to express themselves. Perhaps the weight of the pain they had experienced along life's journey forced them to place a shield around their innermost feelings. Protection of their heart

was their only defense and/or survival. I cannot and will not attempt to speak for them. My desire is to only share the best of these men as only I know it.

As the proud friend and confident to thousands of men when I am graced to be in their presence, I listen for the gift I am to receive. The gift of the person through their experiences; their fears, their joys, their hopes, dreams and desires; their longing for a future that reflects them. Men have a tendency to be much more sensitive than what they appear to be. However the listener or receiver of their reality must be open to 'hear' it. Perhaps men are guarded for the very reason that is stated above, the psychological ramifications. It seems that when a person, any person only half-lives the gifts they are given society is missing out.

When a man is made to believe their emotions are not authentic or that caring for and about themselves is vain, how can we expect for our men to be honest in their communications? They are taught not to be honest within their own body or psyche. Our families, the communities, the environment says silently and verbally "Oh no Men do not behave as such." Again where is this written and more importantly who wrote this? We become suspicious of the man who admires his image in the mirror. Our language is not supportive or encouraging. We continually tear each other down, especially our men folks.

My deepest hope is that all of humanity, particularly our precious men, can look into their mirror with utmost appreciation for who they are as human beings. I would offer my appreciation for the balance that men bring to humanity. I would wish that all men saw the same Love that I see when I look at them. There is no force that must be rendered; no unusual achievement must be earned. What I see when I look at you, my brother, is honorable and respectable. I see a worthy soul. I accept you as you are. There is no battle to be fought or won. No hills to climb or valleys to cross. You are my friend, my chosen confidant, my hero in shining armor.

You are my strong, loving energy that complement my feminine energy. You are my gentle companion in this life. I love you just as you are! There is no competition between us. There is only Love and acceptance. We each have our role to perfect in this thing called life.

I honor your life, your vision and your dreams. I pray I can be whatever you need for me to be to accomplish your dreams. Please feel free to tell me that which you need from me. I will honor your space, your peace and you. I am here to be one with you, not to be confrontational. I am not here to use you up and toss you aside as a nuisance to me. I love YOU, my male energy. I love the man I see in the mirror. You are that you are!

I will hold you up in the highest of light and energy as you reach and touch that Star, your Destiny. My prayer is that you look with Pride and Respect at the Man In Your Mirror!! May you be blessed forever more with assurance that within you is the greatest man ever known to you!! You are the prize....

Internalized self-hatred....

W.E.B. Dubois made a statement to the effect that the human soul cannot be forever chained up or restricted. That when a person is intent on rising up that they shall. I believe W.E.B. Dubois was speaking to the internal psychology of our thinking as well as the external language we use on a daily basis. When we make a sincere choice to rise up and leave behind all that is beneath our heightened awareness, there is no stopping us. We are like a locomotive running along the tracks of life; determined to reach our destination. Even the 'little engine that could' would be successful!

When we know that we are the captains of our own vessels (bodies), we will not allow lack and limitation to be a part of our consciousness. We have the ability to overcome internalized self-hatred. There is no stopping you once you have chosen your path. It is that point along the road that you begin to appreciate what is reflected in your mirror.

The thought for me becomes is it the survival or struggle of the fittest? When we take a deep long look into our past history it will surely cause you to stop if just for a moment to reflect on the characteristics of our fore-fathers and fore-mothers. It is when the struggle within ceases that the masculine energy can fully emerge and manifest itself. The masculine energy is powerful indeed. No struggle is needed. Simply allow.

I am familiar with two very interesting historical perspectives of people, of human beings.

The African history is one that is alive with unquestionable disgrace and abuse of a people. I have journeyed to the Mother Land and have seen ... more importantly 'felt' the holding cells which store-housed humans in the most horrid and hideous surroundings. The humans that were placed and forced into these cells were literally stripped of their dignity, humanness and self-worth. The slave dungeons in Elimina, Ghana, West Africa have a peculiar odor that will probably last forever because it represents such a repulsive time in world history. I felt the ancestral energy of Africa. It may well have been due to my sensitivities around this subject however I did not venture into this to 'feel' like those held in captivity! Yet I did!! It was suffocating it was draining the life force right out of my body. Can you just imagine how they must have felt back then? It was difficult to remain inside the dungeons but I felt I owed that to the ancestors, to my ancestors. What a horrific crime against humanity. It was hard to imagine even in barbaric cultures how this could have happened, yet it did. I still 'feel' the essence of life lived out in those dungeons of Elmina.

When you are inside these dungeons, you witness the stains left from urine and feces from the captives. The stains from their bodily waste are still visible on the walls! The horror and pain one can immediately feel is our connection to those souls that were housed there. These human beings were held captive were forced to eliminate their bodily waste while being housed with others. Everyone were made to urinate and have bowel movements in the common area of the cells! Oh my, what inhumane treatment! No dignity, no self-respect, no care for the rights of the person. Treated like property and animals.

Can you picture for yourself the thousands of bodies crammed together, co-mingling, spreading disease and illness due to the unhealthy and unsanitary conditions? It was not difficult to understand how this could have killed all the captives had that been their fate. Yet many survived that repugnant situation. They survived only to face yet another tragedy upon another until the conquest was complete.

There were many brutal beatings of the bodies of these individuals... these human beings. Some were lynched, some drowned, and some simply did not survive. The disease killed many souls. But then came the water voyage. Yes West Africa sits on the Atlantic Ocean and the people were accustomed to the water ways. Actually some made their living from fishing and other water industries. But they did not know the water in this capacity!

Yet no one could imagine what laid ahead of those captured. When you visit the slave dungeons in Elmina Ghana, the tour guides will initially tell you, the visitor, of their active part in the slave trade and ask for your forgiveness of their ancestors' participation. Families lost. Cultures destroyed. Languages vanished. Livelihoods changed forever. A people raped of their birthrights. A people stolen from home.

This is a life changing event. I would hope that the experience would tug at the heart of any person who was consciously alive while making this journey. If you can allow yourself to be transported back in time via your energy, you can connect with the vibrations of those who were held captive. You literally feel the pain, the shame, the molestation, the horrific treatment; you sense the nightmare that took place in this environment.

So one would wonder how a person or a descendant comes away without being affected or effected by these traumatic experiences. Is this the start, the birthplace of PTSD (Post Traumatic Stress/Slave Disorder)? To be ripped away from your birthplace, your family or your native tongue must have a lasting impact. The survivors were forced into learning a new language to be able to communicate with others. They were forced to denounce their mere existence as they knew it. To be ashamed of their identity. To never acknowledge the place they knew as home. How can this ever be resolved to honor those humans whose very existence cost them their lives in the creation of a land unknown to them?

On another focus, I have had the pleasure of receiving knowledge from the Holocaust Museum, the Museum of Tolerance in Los Angeles. It was the same brutality and harm caused by a few on a larger portion of the population. It left me weeping. My heart ached. This place that honored those lost to the Holocaust was incredible. Such a history lesson.

So this horrendous treatment is not restricted to any one demographics, yet we hold that energy in our bodies from our ancestors. It is no wonder, especially for our men, that we have a difficult time looking into our mirror and being able to accept the image we see looking back at us. The men were for the most part those most actively involved in the bloodshed and inhumane treatment of those held captive. Or at least that's how it's been portrayed. Not attempting to make anyone wrong or responsible, stating the facts as I have seen through the account of history.

I remember seeing at the Museum of Tolerance the pictures of all the women who were brutally beaten, killed and dumped in the ditches alongside the roads. Their bodies naked and bloody. Pictures of pregnant women who were brutally attacked and killed. Women who jumped with their babies from second story buildings to save their child from the horrors of their time. This gave me some appreciation of what Jewish people may have encountered under the monarchy of Hitler.

I can see the faces of the people that were photographed and that were on display. Sometimes the pictures and images are daunting. Hard to accept that we are capable of mistreating other humans so badly, so horribly. My peek into the history of the Jewish people provided me a more complete understanding of the atrocities that they too had to overcome.

Their migration to the USA was achieved by the strong and the brave. As with the Africans that survived the voyage on those slave ships that carried thousands. Too many carried as cargo to the New Land of opportunity.

It did not matter where you settled once you hit American soil. The Original inhabitants of this land were what we now call Native American Indian, a nation of native folks. From the stories in our history books, this land of North America was taken forcibly away from these indigenous people. Perhaps not literally but how do you explain; violence and wars, corruption and control? There are always losers in battles, lives are always lost in wars. And there will forever be scars that are unseen. The mental and emotional scarring that occurs when a person witness the killing of another human is forever etched in the memory.

I have Choctaw Indian blood that runs through my veins. I have German blood that runs through my veins. I have French blood that runs through my veins. I have African blood that runs through my veins. I, like so many others, have a mixed cocktail of ancestry. And within my body is housed conflicting energies perhaps. Or perhaps this mixture gives light to my ability to write about the deeds of some of my ancestors. The misdeeds, if you will.

Yet I love and appreciate all of humanity. Knowing that only when we accept the truth of the past will it set us free to live in peace and acceptance in this the present moment. We always have a choice of the thoughts we think and the actions we take. We can also change those behaviors when we determine they no longer benefit us. Our thoughts are of our own doing. This is the single energy that no one can sabotage unless we give that power, our power away to an outside influence. Many were held captive or prisoner, and many did not allow their mind or thoughts to be poisoned by or with hate.

Be it Brooklyn or Birmingham, New Orleans or New Brunswick, Long Beach NY or Long Beach California, we are each worthy of living a life free of destruction and self-hatred. We must acknowledge the negative emotions and harm existing in our psyche. The unresolved emotional traumas are the villains behind our inability to lovingly gaze into our mirror with complete acceptance and gratitude for the person we now face!

Self-hatred is not some lofty, make-believe terminology. It is as real today as ever. The reasons are plentiful. However I am asking for you to begin the process that would allow you to heal those broken places. Heal the broken places in your heart or your soul. My desire is for you to look with appreciation and gratitude at yourself in a full-length mirror with delight and joy. I believe we can achieve this one small step at a time.

Be willing to take that first step into a brighter future. There may be pain and anguish there. The journey to rid yourself of these hold-backs is so worth the risk. Simply take the first step! As you do, you will discover that each subsequent step is made easier by the courage you display in your forward movement. Have faith that each step will be guided from a deep place within. There is no need to fear that your journey will not be completely unfolded if you just keep moving one step at a time with faith.

Be brave and secure in knowing that the end, the prize of victory will be so great that you will immediately know the value in the journey cannot be denied nor stripped away from you.

You are that man in the mirror, the one that Michael Jackson sung about. You have the power to change the man in your mirror. No one outside of you can do it for you. Nothing outside of you is capable of enriching or increasing your value. What you ultimately think about you is your choice. You can believe that you are made in wholeness, with value and worth. Or you may choose to think otherwise. Remember if what you think no longer serves you and your higher good, you are always permitted to change your thoughts. You may think a new thought at any given time.

In the role as a leader, husband or father you are inclined to help change others for their good. The best way to help others change is by changing yourself, in hopes that your influence and your examples will be a model and inspiration of human excellence.

I see you as a unique, unrepeatable Masterpiece! Individualized Beauty! Creative Genius! You are and can have all that you claim as yours. There is no lack or limitation in this vast abundant Universe. You are capable of thinking your way out of or into newness. You are part of this wondrous global planet of humans. You are worthy to be called by your rightful name. Yes you possess self-love, self-appreciation, self-integrity and self-identification. It is inside of you.

Look at it observing YOU in the mirror! You are the King of the animals; you are the Captain of your vessel; You my dear have dominion over all the earth. Your Spirit knows this to be true and is rejoicing in your reading these words. Your soul is crying out to you to be all that you desire to be**…now!**

WITHIN US

Our true meaning, our purpose, our importance is 'within' us. We shall never find it outside of us. It is not out there some-where, some mysterious place:

- God is not up in the sky or heaven. God lives inside of you, heaven is available to you right now.
- A lover cannot define you or complete you. You are complete within yourself, all by yourself.
- Food may provide temporary comfort but in the long run if not handled with wisdom can get out of control and cause severe problems.
- Working too much and too long is an addiction
- Status, initials, titles cannot make nor define you. You are already more than enough.
- Material things and toys are not a source to define your personhood.

How often do we miss our opportunity to define for ourselves who we are? We are led to believe that this job is always the responsibility of someone else; a parent, a teacher, an elder, the religious leader. Yet at some point in our maturity we arrive at a place of self-realization and description.

We have learned the lessons of childhood and immaturity. We can cite our likes and dislikes; we can in definitive terms explain our goals. We get to set our own mark of excellence. Yet many of us have allowed the standards set by others to tell us who we are. We dare not to achieve more than 'they' say we can do; whoever you decide the 'they' are.

What would happen if we each were given the 'inalienable right' to define our strengths and our gifts and our courage points?

Others will always feel more powerful to know 'what you should do with your life'. And that is okay also, that is if you do not accept someone else's opinion is your barometer of 'who you are'. What if you stopped trying to be someone you are not and have no desire to become? What if you really do know what is best for you? What if God, the Infinite Intelligence granted you with all the wisdom of who you are deep within your cells, within your Divine DNA?

Look into your mirror and marvel at the awesome person you perceive. That person has every right to be here, present in totality right now.

You only need to accept that estimation of who you are, if you are not strong enough within to define yourself. I would urge you to accept that the Most High breathed life into YOU with every right that is bestowed upon every other living human being. Many that would be are not, not here among the living. But you are! You survived and are still here among the living. Your life matters. Your life counts!

Most systems are built to ensure you never realize the fullness of who you are. That is what the movie "The Secret" and "What The Bleep?" are telling us. The rationalization was that to keep humans from living out their power, you make them believe there is something missing from them and that you have the answer. Whoever 'you' may be. 'You' may be the right book, the right neighborhood, the right city, the right college, etc. And different concepts are created to help you master your **'lack of something'** which proves their product is what you require to become _____, whatever the underlying thing is you say you need to be successful.

Yet sometimes we attempt to be something or someone that we are not meant to be nor become. We do not utilize our natural strengths and powers. We spend endless time, money and resources to fix something about us that is not even a match for us. When we can match our passion (strengths) with our energy we will raise to the top each and every time.

We are not created to be perfect in every area. Most of us have one extremely commanding talent or gift. I believe many of us have several gifts and we only choose to develop one. That dominant power can create massive benefits when we allow ourselves to be immersed in it.

Do not imitate the way of this world, but be transformed by the renewing of your minds, that you may discern what is that good and acceptable and perfect will of God. Romans 12:6. Holy Bible, Lamsa's Aramaic Translation

STAGE 8

What Is Beauty?

WHAT REALLY INFLUENCES OUR THOUGHTS?

OK so today I am having a discussion with a College educated African-American female of about 30 years of age. This female actually is duo-degreed, you know she is heavy, got 2 acknowledgements that she is smart.

Anyway, this is what happened…..she made mention of the hard red dirt in Georgia. I was so excited because I had just seen the documentary, **The Trails of Tears, Cherokee Legacy.** And I mentioned that to her, thinking we could have a conversation of what happened to the Native Indians living in what is now called the United States of America. The red dirt was due to all the blood shed by the Cherokee Indians which stained the earth permanently to remind us of this travesty, that it was brutality at its worst. Keep in mind that the two of us are of the same nationality.

To my utter amazement, after she informed me how knowledgeable she was about the Cherokees, she boldly stated she had mixed views on the subject. What, 'mixed views'? Right about now I am confused and hoping that she will soon shine some light on the subject and thus correct what I was feeling. She continued to say that the Cherokee tried too hard to be just like the whites of that time, marrying white women, going to their schools, etc. She strongly felt that the Cherokee were somehow responsible for the tremendous loss of life that was experienced and being forced out of their sacred native land.

And before I could stop the words I asked my fine extremely intelligent, intellectual and educated friend, "Well what do you think about black or African-American women who abuse themselves with chemicals to straighten their hair to look like or assimilate the lighter complexion folks?" I asked this question because she had already explained to me how she had lost so much of her own hair using perms and other chemicals to 'keep her hair in order'. Her hair is so badly damaged that the very hair follicle appears empty, which may very well prevent her from ever being able to grow healthy hair on her scalp again. I said, "To me that demonstrates the same type of desire to be like the 'white person', and that we hate ourselves so much that we would rather be bald than to wear our hair natural!"

I remember the day before, she had asked me if she could grow 'dread locs' on her permed, chemically relaxed hair, please understand or visualize this if you can. Her hair line is far, inches, removed from its natural placement. She understands how she has abused her hair but states she just have to do what she has to do to look presentable!!! OK then so be it.

So my point is this, Is this too not trying to look or be like a white person? She fell silent on me, no response whatsoever.

The Cherokee Indians were terrorized by the European just like the Africans in an attempt to create a so-called 'white' race. Both were removed from their homeland, both thought to be less than a human. You must be thinking right about now, whose standards were these assumptions being made upon? Who gave them or granted them the right to dictate who is or is not human?

I am **not** racist, very outspoken but never racist. I am a mixed breed, a delicious mixture of African, Choctaw Indian, French and German!

The more I learn about the formation of these United States of America (united by notoriously violent ways/acts) that was never taught in the educational system – the more I wonder about life, liberty and justice for all and what could have possibly meant the greedy, unscrupulous and murderous man that decided to annihilate so many other cultures and living human beings to create a 'test tube race'!!!

I'm just saying........

Why do we have to dig and find scandalous workings of the government and former Presidents to really know the truth? Why is the truth hidden from our sight?

We are being pacified with distractions; like all the trinkets and gadgets that the media 'insists' you must have in order to be somebody. This form of manipulation has taken years, generations to perfect. Back in the early 1960's was the introduction of personal sized TV dinners, teaching the concept of individuality. Before its creation people sat with each other or neighbors joined a family and sat together to sup together. Then came the microwave, fix it in a hurry mentality set in very quickly after that (get the pun?).

We just keep riding the coat tails of this insanity, this ludicrous thinking. The music cannot even be understood unless its blasting. Our young boys are walking around showing their butts and think nothing is wrong or abnormal about it. Ask why they do it and they will tell you because everyone else is doing it. I ain't mad, I just wish someone, and especially a young person will gather enough courage to stand up for the sanity of the populous. I just want one person to tell me why they do this. Why wear any pants at all? What's next?

We are being hood winked, sold a bill of goods that is damaging and destroying this very precious commodity, life. We continue to let other people tell us how to think and what to wear, what to spend our money on and listen to the idiots they have claimed as our spokespersons. When a large portion of our entertainment is being controlled by someone other than us, there is a huge danger involved in what the message will be to the listeners.

Oh my, what an eye-opener for me. Just to think with just a comment about the 'hard red dirt' in Georgia and the flood gates of rational thinking began to flow forward.

(note: The Trail of Tears is a part of American history where thousands upon thousands of Cherokee Indians were killed by soldiers, diseases, rotten food, forced off their land, made to walk hundreds of miles to another state so that Georgians could mine the gold found in the mountains of Georgia. Read the story for yourself or watch the documentary produced by a Cherokee.)

AND BEAUTY IS.....

In America there exists a huge discrepancy about what is 'beauty' –

For darker hue complexions the divide is much grander with few examples that are unique. Most examples resemble a chocolate covered 'Barbie' instead of incorporating distinctive features. The unique characteristics of Asian, Hispanic, Latin or African are not generally depicted as beautiful, if depicted in major media at all.

However in 2013 several movies made a splash with the movie industry displaying African American females in very important leading and supporting roles that caught the attention of the Award Industry. Lupita Nyong'o, for instance, won Best Supporting Actress 2014 for her role in **'12 Years A Slave'**. Several other women displayed a more natural appearance in their roles during 2013, like Halle Barry in **'The Call'**, Yolanda Ross and LisaGay Hamilton in **'Go For Sisters'**, Naomie Harris in **'Mandela Long Walk to Freedom'** and Jennifer Hudson in **'Winnie'**, just to name a few. In 2013, Ava DuVernay, made history as the first African-American woman to win Best Director at Sundance for her film **'Middle of Nowhere'**, and Iyanla Vanzant who has consistently displayed her natural beauty with pride. Yet the deep ebony melanin matched with the natural hairstyle worn by Lupita Nyong'o, were noted and glamorized as the jewels they are.

In a speech given by Lupita Nyong'o, her words are enlightening, meaningful and inspiring especially to younger females growing up in an age where they have instant access to information via the internet. The media is quick to advertise for the sole purpose of selling their products to the unsuspecting female who has bought into the notion that she is somehow unattractive without this particular product.

Lupita explains her trials and tribulations, her not being able to completely comprehend what people were telling her about her beauty or lack thereof. Lupita's words speaks volumes to the older generation of women who silently wished they could be accepted by society sometimes by their own birth family. The reality of some families' harshness can be attributed to the fact that perhaps they lacked a point of reference for beauty.

Lupita talks about her dark skin as if it were a curse. I remember my dad telling me that when he worked for the Los Angeles Department of Public Works his job was to paint various objects. Sometimes his assignments would be in rather unusual places. On this occasion he was painting in a rather public place and a small white child walked up to him and looked bewildered. After the small child had starred at him for several minutes the little boy finally rubbed his, my father, face then looked at his hand. With amazement the little boy said, "It doesn't rub off?" with a questioned look on his face. My father was not amused with this and it stayed in his memory. My father would not explain any further about this incident. But his face showed all the evidence of a wounded soul. Here he was simply performing his job so that he could provide for his family. This little boy with an inquisitive nature wanted to help him out by rubbing the darkness off of his face. I can only imagine what my dad must have felt.

He and my mother moved to the big city to escape the small-mindedness of the little country place where they grew up in Louisiana. Some things just did not seem to change for him. He still faced a sense of not being completely accepted just for who he was, a man working on an honest job to feed and house his family.

And I remember how popular the bleaching creams were. Lupita talks about one brand called Dencia's Whitenicious and although I never heard of that particular brand. Nadinola bleaching cream was very popular when I was growing up. Black women purchased and used this cream, praying that their skin would become lighter so they could be more acceptable in everyone's eyesight. I believe especially their own. I know at least one of my cousins was religious in her efforts to lighten her skin. Without fail every single day she used Nadinloa on her face and silently prayed for lighter skin.

This is an International crime against humanity. The chemicals used in these bleaching creams can cause cancer, infertility and other health issues for the people who use them consistently. These health concerns are not discussed in the media. Why? Possible the cosmetics companies have a decisive input on what is reported to the general public about the safety of their product. Lives are being damaged both physically and mentally. The start for the need of this product is because people are believing the hype that they are ugly and need help to be a prettier person. How can so many people be deceived into wanting to look like someone else? I do not have the answer to this question. Just wanted to raise that question that perhaps the discussions can be had and someone will figure it out and make a change for the acceptance of who we are, exactly as we are!

I sincerely thank Ms. Lupita Nyong'o for having the courage to tell her story without apology. That this speech is even necessary says a lot about what is projected on the screens of our consciousness as this so-called imagery known as 'beauty'. When we leave so many people out of the equation, how does that impact their lives? Is the incidence of mental health problems including suicidal actions increased by this visual depiction of a false reality? Its all an illusion folks.

In America, as Nigerian author Chimamanda Ngozi Adichie tells her story, there exists a race consciousness that is not evident in other parts of the world. It is quite amusing to hear her speak of 'being a non-American Black in America' and how that communicates various human rights as an outsider looking in. She says the race relations are layered into a race, culture and class pyramid. The American media plays such a huge part in identifying this separatism. Our national news stations will almost always depict the villains in all crimes as being a black person. I know this to be true for myself and have stopped watching network TV news for that very reason. Chimamanda calls this experience 'Identity displacement' what an appropriate terminology for this phenomenal.

As for African American women, our mirror of beauty and acceptance has long been smashed into a million pieces, not just cracked. Many do not even look any longer. Their vision is obscured by this warped sense of beauty being depicted in most visual media segments.

Perhaps the self-hatred began with the first shipload of slaves from Africa. The Slave Trade <u>had</u> to insist on and rob the beauty, the culture, the pride of the people it needed or intended to misuse to their advantage. No human can be subjected to erasing their self-pride without a planned systematic approach.

It is time to reclaim the royal elegance of our status! To know rightfully who we are, a proud people who do not need to mimic or imitate someone else's physical characteristics to appreciate our self-love and self-dignity. We can no longer tolerate the demeaning of our humanness. Our Ancestors loathed who they were because it meant survival for them (see the willie lynch letter, non-capitalized letters intended). It seems the spell has not been broken, we must **not** allow this to continue into our future generations.

Without others acknowledging and/or verifying our inherent beauty we can accomplish this for ourselves. We can boast of our own unique beauty marks; our wide juicy, kissable lips, our curvaceous hips and thighs, our un-limited naturally kinky glorious hair, our many shades of black and brown hues and our pure magnificent essence is to be celebrated. We must do this for ourselves.

In an excerpt from "Talking Back: Thinking Feminist" author bell hooks writes an essay on 'Straightening Our Hair'. She delves deeply into the psychological and sociological aspects garnering her tribal and familial rituals of why we suffered to press and remove the natural beautiful curls and texture of our incredible hair. Her article will have you smiling with memories and hopefully thinking about habitual things we unconsciously did in the name and sake of beauty.

All people, all women have a right to be accepted in their own body form and shape. Whatever she looks like does not matter as long as she is healthy. Not all skinny people are healthy, some are simply skinny. By the same token not all weighty people are unhealthy.

Let our lives be that of balance; spiritual, physical, mental and emotional. We deserve that balance and we must demand that for ourselves, our children, our grandchildren and our neighbors everywhere around the globe.

We must stand up with and for one another. Solidarity is the strength in changing some of the bigotry from centuries past (passed). We can define our beauty for who we are today. We can say loudly that we accept the uniqueness of our being-ness. We can shout that we are Beautiful, Capable, Wondrous, Lovable individuals. It is our voice and we should use it to lift us UP!

Please accept that beautiful image you see staring you in the face when you gaze into your mirror. She/he is grand and wonder-filled. You are an unrepeatable miracle of life! Look again and find the courage to welcome who you see into your daily existence. Walk with this person, talk with this person, share your innermost dreams with this person. You and this person are ONE!

AGING –

Aging is not appreciated nor welcomed in America. Have you seen all the commercials and ads in the magazines or on the web? We succumb to Botox, plastic surgery and any number of procedures to maintain (as the advertisers would claim) a youthful appearance!

Why would we desire to dishonor the maturity phase of our life? Why must we continually fight against accepting change as a natural state of sequences in life? Why do we dread getting older? Why have we accepted this is not a desired state of being?

The statistics claim more and more people are entering into what has been coined the Baby Boomer generation resulting in large numbers of older Americans living longer than our ancestors. If this is true, why not embrace with all the learnings we have and become so much more than we ever thought was possible? Is this not an invitation to be greater?

Are we attempting to become more 'perfect' by denying the undeniable fact we are already made perfect by the Creator of all living things?

I am amused by our celebrities who promote *no wrinkles or facial lines, no drooping or sagging body parts*. I do know this is possible with the correct exercise regimen and proper eating habits. However, we are tempted to stay on an unhealthy lifestyle yet wish for magical results. Weight loss and tighter skin is the result of proper care of the body temple, at any age.

What is this quest for the Fountain of Perpetual Youth all about? Why do we fear aging? What do we gain by not accepting the natural process of life? Can we maintain our youth by our mental thoughts, even when the outer shows signs of maturity? What's worse than getting older, no a better question is, what is the opposite of getting older?

MEN –

Man measures time; but time is a gift from God. **By Reggie Smith**

The attitude became a behavior, which begat a character defect, which begat the consequences that fueled the energetic dissonance that disrupted the harmonic flow of my life. I was not only blocking my blessings, I was missing them.

There are things I want to get done in this lifetime, but I would be remiss if I did not enjoy this now moment. I still feel like a youthful person. My body will age, but my spirit remains young. I consider my "soul" to be the recorder of all things eternal, like a hard drive, and my mind is my random access memory, or RAM, limited in scope but powerfully designed. I interface with others on the intranets of my social circles, or the worldwide web of universal spirit. My sense and experience show that we can effect healing for our human conditions when we operate on a plane of existence that is connected to the "Now". In order to be "here and now" I have to momentarily silence the past and the future and FOCUS!

One constant in my life has been my conscious observation of the movie that is my life. I remember, as best I can, the experiences that I have had along the continuum we call "time"… You are a co-star, supporting cast member, or simply an extra. I take my cues from the producer/director … God.

Somehow, all these storylines take their place on a common space/time continuum we call life. Most of us are consumed with playing our own part. I always try to remember though, "It's one thing to play the role; and another to let the role play you".

Compared to girls, research shows that boys in the U.S. are more likely to be diagnosed with a behavior disorder, prescribed stimulant medications, fail out of school, binge drink, commit a violent crime, and/or take their own lives.

Jennifer Siebel Newsom's documentary film, **The Mask You Live In,** asks: As a society, how are we failing our boys?

Watching the trailer I noted this segment titled **The Most Damaging Words You Can Tell Your Son**

- Don't cry, stop the tears
- Stop with all the emotions
- Don't be a wimp
- Get some 'balls'

Coach Joe Ehrman, a former NFL player believes 'The 3 most destructive words for a man to tell a boy is 'Be A Man'.

Ashanti Branch, Educator and Youth Advocate summarizes it this way 'Our children prepare their 'mask' every morning as they prepare for school and they don't know how to take the mask off'

Are we or do we live in a society that does not value the totality of being human with emotions as William Saafir eluded to in his Preface to **"All My Men."** *"At the very foundation of intellectual growth and human progress is the healthy use of the five senses. These five senses, given proper expression, will lead us to higher and higher refinement. Ultimately, with time and plenty of help, the human being evolves to become a very highly sensitive creature.*

The highest expression of these sensitivities is that of love. Love is the well from which all other sensitivities spring forth. Love is the purest of all human expressions. Evidence of this purity is the fact that you have to love a thing before you can give your whole mind (your whole self) to it. It is this unselfish, unrestrained giving of yourself to the things you value that allows your excellence to manifest itself."

Suppressed feelings and emotions are directly linked to mental health imbalances. However we as a society we shun the very issues which we have created. As a society, we only want to hear about the feelings and emotions <u>after</u> they have become an issue causing health problems with a person. If we took that same energy and showed compassion with a young boy, avoiding the trap of making him feel less masculine perhaps we can save our young men.

Suicide becomes an option that youngsters consider; the statistics prove that point, 3 or more boys commit suicide on any given day in the U.S. Well if those numbers aren't staggering to you then perhaps that is the very reason why so many young people are taking their own lives. They lack compassion and wisdom from the elders, especially the older men. This not only applies to fathers, this applies to all male figures. You can always be a role model or big brother to a younger man.

The terminology 'Man UP' has some heavy connotations attached. Probably most important is what does that mean to a young boy who is simply attempting to figure out the hormonal changes going on in his body? Remember as we approach puberty and adolescence, the entire world changes, yet sometimes the older folks forget. And a boy can never be a 'man' until he becomes one.

Adults let the children be children. Allow the grown folks to handle and take care of adult business. Your son did not sign up for 'daddy duty' or 'man of the house' duty. Please stop with this nonsense. Thank you.

Rev. Leevahn Smith believes 'Being self-defined and self-determined disempowers the system of oppression…loving yourself enough to take control of your life. This implies that high self-esteem is required.' As we studied *'Struggling Against Oppression in the African American Church by LGBTQ People Seeking Justice'*, this statement from my notes sums up the context of our learning experience.

'As a result, we continued to give birth to self-hatred and could not trust those who reminded us of ourselves. We were stuck in an unhappy, lonely and depressing place. Homophobia in the African American church drove us to dark and risky places while participating in unhealthy and risky behaviors became familiar practices.'

This self-hatred is a dangerous emotion to fill up your consciousness. People do all sorts of things when full of self-hate, not only to themselves but to others as well. Self-hatred can have a deafening effect on you and how you navigate through life. Self-hate can perpetuate situations which causes harm to self and others. A person with self-hatred can be known for abusing any number of substances; food, prescription medicines, excessive work, etc.

This philosophy is not new. And with reality in mind it stands to reason that this condition with our youth should be one we focus our attention to minimize if not completely destroy from their lifestyle. It serves no reason for us not to take action and assist these young people with fully living out their life in complete acceptance.

Switched At Birth by **Pedro Silva** via www.theroofleschurch.wordpress.com blog

When I was a child, I had a difficult time accepting my name... It was as if I was aware that this was not really my name, but rather something people were calling me just to get my attention. My experience was that when no one called out to me I was fully being who I am. . . I was reduced to whatever the callers thoughts were about this "Pedro".

In the book of Jeremiah, God tells the young prophet to be, "Before I formed you in the womb I knew you, and before you were born I consecrated you." What if that is true for all of us? What if the person God knows us to be--the person we were when we came into this world--is the person we were always intended to be. What if "underneath" all of these layers of association that person still remains, untouched and undefiled by the world that knows not who we are? And what if accessing that true being that you are is just a thought away? These are questions I asked myself when I first heard this scripture. I decided then and there that I wanted to know myself as the person God knows even before a body was associated with my being. My strongest desire is to know myself as I am. And the closest route I can think of to know this is to go back to the Source.

Friends, We are all children of God. Despite how we might perceive ourselves right now or the conditions that may be appearing in our consciousness we are not less than the person we were when we came here. We cannot <u>uncreate</u> ourselves. We can only choose to deny the gift that God the Giver gives. Fortunately, it is never too late to be born into God's wealthy family. If you don't know yourself to be a child of the Creator of All then perhaps you might consider that you were switched at birth. I know that it may difficult to accept. The greatest temptation to accepting this gift is the temptation to blame those who came before us--those who may have involuntarily led us to forget who we are because they forgot who they are. But this is folly, because to blame anyone is to deny ourselves the power to reclaim our true lives and our inheritance. This is the light of Jesus' teachings on forgiveness, loving our enemies, and giving to those who cannot repay us. In order to see our innocence, we must accept the innocence of our brothers and sisters, which in some small way sets a portion of them free from the lie of who they aren't and sets ourselves free to the same degree.

"Forgive us our debts as we forgive our debtors." Imagine that in this one statement you are graced with the gift to set us all free."

I have used almost the entire text of this blog from one of my God-sons, Rev. Pedro Silva. After reading it for the first time I thought to myself what a 'Divine" intervention to receive this magnificent piece so eloquently written from a male perspective. I trust and know that while in the midst of writing this book, awesome words and revelations would come to me through others.

I have shared in this section on the male energy some outstanding views from others who are on this same journey of awakening and educating

Both Leevahn and Pedro cautions us disempower those who would seek to cause us harm by not knowing who we are. Let us educate and strengthen our inner self to trust we are unshakable, trustworthy people living an incredulous life on Mother Earth. Let us not be thrown off course but be unyielding to the unnecessary road blocks and detours. Let us help our fellow human being to be all that they can be also. Let us lift UP and not tear down this human race. We each have a significant part of history. We each are an integral aspect.

FINAL STAGE

Positive Spiritual Upliftment

Use the following affirmations to encourage and increase your feelings of self worth and worthiness.

I AM WORTH IT!

Today you have permission to boast that you are worth it! You are worth a grand life, living in abundance and prosperity in all areas. You are worth accomplishing that dream. You are worth the unconditional love of others. You are worth peace and harmony. You are worth the time and effort. You are worth life and breath. You are worthy!

Stand up straight! Shoulders back with head held very high! Strut with the air of confidence that acknowledges your acceptance that you are worth it! You are worth every good thing.

You have been created like none other. Your life is a miracle and you are an unrepeatable expression of The Most High. You are worth this gift of life. You are worth living. Your life has meaning and purpose. Your life has value. Yes You are worth it!

I keep repeating to myself today that I Am Worthy. I deserve to live a full and happy life. I Am heir to this earthly Kingdom. I Am deserving of the best life has to offer. I Am Worthy! I Am Worth It!

Yes God, I accept my value. I give Thanks for my placement in Your Kingdom. Yes God, I have been appointed by You to be an example of Unconditional Love and Acceptance. Yes God, I Am Worthy of full expression of my divinity and connection to The Source. Yes God, I am ready to shout and proclaim – I Am Worth It!!!

I say this today as my prayer out into the Universe.

I say this today as my Affirmation and Confirmation.

My thoughts, words and actions today reflect my confidence in knowing I Am Worth It!

I Am Living proof of the Goodness of The Creator!

I AM WORTH IT!

THANKFUL

Today we are centered in being Thankful. We are Thankful for the very gift of this life and all it has for us.

We are Thankful to The Creator for creating us just as we are. We are Thankful to live in such a time as this, full of wonder and modern technology. I can think of someone and within seconds I can send an email letting them know just how much I care about them. Although I still enjoy writing letters because it shows I thought enough to sit down with a pen and paper and compose something special just for that person.

We are Thankful for each and every thing that is currently present in our lives. We are Thankful because our thoughts have placed them here with us. We are Thankful because at any given time we can change the appearance of things by choosing to change our thoughts. We are Thankful that The Creator designed us that way, divine and perfect.

We are Thankful for our earthly parents that chose to participate in our coming forth in this world. We are Thankful for their presence and contributions to who we are now. We give Thanks for however they have shown up for us, it is exactly as it is, just for our growth.

We are Thankful for the multitudes that have graced our path, giving us precisely those things we desired at the time, whether they are blessings or lessons. Each came with their unique gift for us.

We simply celebrate each day with Thanksgiving. We give Thanks as our demonstration to The Most High of our sincere gratitude for our gift of life.

Thanks God. Thanks Allah. Thanks Jehovah. Thanks DAO. Thanks Buddha. Thanks, Thanks, Thanks.

The Most High is worthy to be PRAISED.

I CHECK MYSELF

Today I check in on myself and determine what it is I am feeling and experiencing in life. Today I pay close attention to my body and how it responds to certain situations and/or people. I know the Spirit that dwells inside of me, knows more than I do and will advise me. All that is needed of me is to be alert and aware of how I react.

I may feel tension around certain groups of people. What are the core beliefs of the people I am with? Is there a match with my inner beliefs? Have I been placed in with this group to learn or teach a lesson? Am I giving my best to this environment?

Is my Spirit joyous when I am doing this? Do the creative juices of self expression run rampant as I am actively involved with this? Would I do this regardless to any other circumstance being present? Do I feel light and carefree while engaged in this activity?

Today I check my true self for understanding how the various situations I find myself in are affecting my Spirit. Today I pay close attention to each encounter. It is my responsibility to do this for myself, to continually check my Spiritual pulse for accuracy. Today I give me what I need, to be in perfect alignment with God's Will for my life.

I check myself with absolute honesty and truth. I remain in integrity with myself each and every step of the way. I am obligated to tell myself the truth, even if what I am experiencing is different from that which I desire to manifest. And I remind myself that wherever I am, it is perfectly okay.

I check myself today with Love and Passion, with Truth and Peace, with Compassion and Forgiveness.

GET UP, GET OUT AND LIVE

Get up with purpose today. Decide your goals for today and succeed in accomplishing each one of them. Make your decisions today that are firmly based in prayer. Begin with a prayer of Thanksgiving for being alive this day. Think on those things that you desire and go to God, asking for guidance and support. When you are clear, proceed with confidence.

Get out into the world today with great enthusiasm. Demonstrate your excitement for life today. Allow your energy to lead you throughout the day. Be Excited! The energy of excitement will lead you into new areas, simply because the Universe is responding to your expectations.

Dare to LIVE this day as never before. Live in full abandonment of what you have done repeatedly in the past. LIVE as if this is the last day for you here on earth. LIVE, knowing that your path is made clear and straight by God, The Omnipotent One. LIVE as if you have no other choice. LIVE, trusting the process of life, accepting all miracles that are being given to you.

Get up, get out and live today! Enjoy the magic of a new dawn of possibilities. Get out and truly smell the awesome fresh air. Inhale it fully. Feel the glory of God in each breath you take. Exhale all the worries and concerns. Let them go out from you. Live today in complete Love and Acceptance. Embrace all others with Unconditional Love. LIVE today in Harmony and Peace.

Others will want what you have, the energy and excitement for life! Be the example today. Set the higher mark this day. Life is fabulous, live like you know it! Life is wonderful, live like you are grateful for this free gift!

I thank God this day. I praise The Creator today. I sing with joy, songs to The Most High. The Creator is my source.

YOUR NATURE

Our very nature is life looking for life. This
is the Oneness, the Unity of God.

God has created you! What an honor! What a privilege! A
Miracle of Supreme Intelligence! You are very special.

Your nature is that of a victorious individual. Your life does have meaning and purpose. You are the descendent of a people that survived and passed their DNA on to you. Regardless to your particular family of origin, there may have been struggle and that all has been removed. You get to set a new course, if that is your desire.

Consider the art of creation that caused you to be alive. In the making of you were five million sperm going after one egg, to fertilize and cause a life to begin. That's right, 5,000,000 sperm looking for the opportunity to create your life! No accident here, only absolute thanks for your life. In the beginning, it was life looking for life to begin another life! Your existence is miraculous.

To extend your life, you serve others. The service of one person to another is God's Law. The act and movement of Unconditional Love sustains this life force. Yes your life has purpose and many have fought to give you this grand opportunity to experience LIFE!

The True Life is that of Harmony and Justice. The True Life is that of Infinite Possibilities and Success. The True Life is Abundant Prosperity in all areas. The True Life is looking towards adding value to other life forms. The True Life is looking for more True Life.

Your nature is LIFE. Life is: Living In Full Expression. Your full expression is that of more life. Your full expression is sharing your unique gifts. Your full expression is being of service to others. Your full expression is victorious, enthusiastic, energetic and thankful.

EYE TO EYE WITH MY SOUL

I stand gazing into the eyes that are looking back at me in the mirror. I see clearly the passion of my soul. I am eye to eye with my own soul! I admire the Spirit that lives forever in my soul. I adore the Awesome, Incredible Presence of God in my soul.

Eye to eye with my soul means I take full responsibility for the things and actions I take. I am solely responsible for my life. All that is present I have created by conscious choice or default, by not making a decision.

What do you see as you gaze into the mirror? Is it hope and joy? Do you really know the depths of your soul? What is that yearning about? What is it that you desire to manifest in your life?

As you look deep into your own soul, give thanks. Be thankful for all that you see. You have come a long way. You are working through your own issues, sometimes it may have been difficult however you are still on the path. This process we call life is glorious indeed. It is filled with wonder, when we choose to view it that way.

Take another look. See the beauty of your Spirit! See the unlimited abundance of Love that is glowing back at you! See the miracle that is manifested as YOU! Love what you see reflected back at you! No changes, no would have or could have, simply LOVE the reflection. Wink at the reflection, flirt with the reflection. Yes, show yourself some LOVE!

I stand admiring the reflection in the mirror. I am eye to eye with my own soul and I appreciate what I feel and see.

I AM AWESOME

Thanks God for my life. My Life is Awesome. I Am Awesome!

To recognize the true essence of The Creator, we must accept that same true essence dwells within us. We must look within ourselves and honor that place of connection to God. We are the earthly expressions of The Most High. The Creator is seen through us. We are each others' Angels. We are God in human form!

To recognize and celebrate this divinity is the way to fully appreciate and give Thanks to the One Source. In each human dwells the same Goodness of God. I recognize and give thanks for the life form that appears on my path each day. I choose to see The Divinity in every person I meet and associate with. I celebrate them wholly.

I Am Awesome is a reflection of my Truth. I Am Awesome is a statement of Whose I Am. I know I Am Awesome.

I give Thanks today. I shout Thanks to the Universe. I shout Thanks to My God. I tremble with knowing that God is protecting and providing for me each and every day. I Am an Awesome creation of The Master Giver.

Yes today I choose to display myself with respect and dignity. I live in integrity and humbleness. My life is indeed a Blessing and for this I give Thanks.

I give Thanks and sing songs of Thanksgiving. I am happy and filled with Joy. I allow the world to see my magnificence. I am Love. I am Peace. I am Harmony. I am Justice. I am all that God has created and intended for me to be.

I know – I AM AWESOME!

YOU ARE WORTHY

You are alive and well, means you are worthy! You are a breathing soul, means that you are worthy. The precious blood that circulates through your body means you are worthy! By simply BE-ing you are worthy!!!

I declare and accept my worthiness right now! I know that my life has meaning, value and worth. I am a deserving human, deserving of all honor, respect and dignity. I choose to not give or compromise myself in any situation. I cherish my self-worth.

I know I Am Worthy because I Am a God-child. I Am heir to the Kingdom of The Creator. My worth has nothing to do with the kind of work I perform or the material possessions I own. My Worth is freely given to me through my life and existence.

I accept I Am worthy through God's Grace and Mercy! I acknowledge all others with this same attribute of Worthiness. We are each the same.

It is my job to recognize the God-presence in every person I encounter. I choose to honor their presence and accept they are worthy souls on this journey of life with me. My life is enriched by the multitudes. My circle of friends is filled with worthy folks. My family represents all worthy individuals. The stranger on the street is a worthy child of God. The meek, sick and shut-in are all worthy folks. The disabled, handicap and challenged are all worthy.

In memory of those that have departed this physical plane, I honor your valued contributions to my existence. I know you are forever a worthy element of this vast Universe.

I add value by accepting and expressing my worthiness. I seek and see worthy folks all around me, everyplace I go. We are all the same.

YOU ARE MORE THAN ENOUGH

Yes, YOU are more than enough!

It is not about the clothes you wear, the designer labels and all. It is not about the fancy car you drive. It is not even about what you do for a living. Nor is it about the family you were born into.

YOU are more than enough because YOU are a Child of God! Your heritage is of royalty, honor, prosperity, abundance, riches and ultimate Joy. Without you having to do one single thing you are entitled to live prosperously and lavishly abundant. This is your inheritance from your Creator.

Right here where I Am I accept my birthright to achieve all that I dare to dream of being and becoming. I know there are no limitations other than the ones I place on myself. I allow the goodness and the Mercy to overtake me completely. I bathe in the vastness of my riches. I am grateful for the abundance. I declare my share is more than sufficient; I overflow with abundance in every area of my life. I give Thanks and proclaim my destiny.

I salute you with My Overflowing Cup! Here's to your success and your greatness. I honor you in achieving all that you have set out to do. I respect your drive and commitment to reaching that unreachable star! To go where you have never allowed yourself to go.

Yes YOU are ready and amply capable of success. YOU are more than enough to achieve your greatest desires and aspirations.

Seize this opportunity to BE ALL THAT YOU DESIRE TO BE!

The Universe is waiting for you. The Universe knows:

YOU ARE MORE THAN ENOUGH

FISHING POND

What are you catching with your fishing pole (consciousness)? What bait (thoughts) are you using? What size is your fishing pond (Faith)?

You can pull/catch the future and bring it into the present. Or you can continue catching the past by not releasing the old worn out tape. It is your choice. When you desire newness, you will gladly relinquish attachment to the past. I can stop the tape of the past and discord it. As long as I find comfort in the familiar, even when it may cause me pain, and stay there, that is my choice.

Today I choose to fish from the pond of unlimited possibilities. I open myself up to visualizing in grand style. I use my gift of imagination and expand it by increasing my vision. I continue with this process of expanding and increasing until it is complete. Then I start over because I know God is in control, which is my Faith. My vision is impaired by my physical knowledge. However, I accept God has more in store for me than I could ever imagine. I do my part by beginning the process and then allowing the Infinite Intelligence to guide and direct me to what and where I am to go. I am ever Thankful for being led by The Most High to my higher state of being and consciousness.

I require a large vessel to hold the fish I catch today. No longer is a small ship large enough to hold my catch. I willingly expand to receive my expected and unexpected good! It is right in front of me, some I see while others are just below the surface waiting for my bait to snag them.

Praises, Praises, Praises. As Praises go Up, Blessings Come Down! I graciously accept them ALL! Thanks God. So Be It!!!

HOW DO YOU SHOW UP?

In the presence of others, do you take the high road of authenticity or gauge how you show up dependent upon on how the others appear? This is sometimes referred to as peer pressure. And you thought that only applied to children, especially teenagers. Well it does not and guess what, the same small children you are saying this to are watching you and how you show up in the company of others.

Do not compromise your values for the sake of belonging. Isn't that what we tell our children? Be a leader not a follower, and there we go following the gang because everyone is doing it. As we get older our gang is broader and is often influenced by what we see on television and what we hear in the music. The community at large becomes our gang, the people we hang out with. In this process do you still honor your truth? Or are you following the crowds, the same crowd we warn our children about?

Actions are always much louder than our words. Our children are watching. How we show up! Are your actions consistent with your values? How do you show up? Is the environment the one who sets the tone of what is fashionable and the latest trend? Are your actions consistent with your words?

Is honesty an admirable value? Yet you lie to others often, in the company of your children? What do you think they are learning that it is okay to lie some of the time, because they hear you doing it? Well if this is how you show up, please do not chastise the children for repeating what you are teaching. Do you holler, scream and curse others when you are upset? But insist upon spanking the child that does the same as you?

How do you show up for yourself? Do you compromise because you feel intimidated by titles or status of others? Regardless of the position in life we are each the same, a child of God.

Respect yourself and show up as the real you all the time!

LEARN TO LOVE YOURSELF

I use the term, 'Learn to Love Yourself' because many of us often leave that to someone else to do for us. Despite what you have thought in the past, you must LOVE yourself before anyone else can truly love you.

To love yourself is to be completely honest with your thoughts and actions towards you. And you do not have to share your inner most thoughts with anyone unless you choose to do so. So what are you really thinking these days? Do you believe you are worthy of the goals and dreams you have for yourself? Are you beautiful by your own standards? Do you experience JOY on a deep soul satisfying level?

You can learn to be 'in love' with you, at all times and through all circumstances. You learn this by simply doing it, without excuse or resistance. Just Love who you have become, all the wonderful lessons you have learned and all the growth you have experienced. Isn't it grand to count it all a blessing? It is your life, your physical existence. It is your heart and your soul that we are celebrating with absolute Joy! Love that person at the deepest levels and watch how much better your life becomes. You are doing it for yourself AND that is reason enough.

Practice giving the best to you this day. They say practice makes perfect. So continue to practice loving your self until you become a master at it. Truly love without any conditions. To love yourself is the greatest gift you can give to you today.

I Love Me today! I truly Love Me today! I Am worthy of LOVE! And I accept Love into my life, beginning with self love. I give myself permission to Love freely, without restraints or limitations. I simply choose to LOVE!

I Am my best friend. I tell myself the truth at all times. I am patient and kind with me. I choose words of support and encouragement with myself. I know I can and I will; it is my choice.

This very day, I WILL LOVE MYSELF
FULLY AND COMPLETELY!

NOTES:

NOTES:

NOTES:

NOTES:

ACKNOWLEDGEMENTS

The following individuals have impacted my life; thoughts and insights from them appear in the writing of this book. With honor I mention their names and titles here:

> A Return to Love – 'Our Deepest Fear' by Marianne Williamson
> The Mask You Live In (Documentary) – Jennifer Siebel Newsom
> Man Measures Time – Reggie Smith (RISE Magazine)
> Reverend Leevahn Smith
> Switched At Birth – Reverend Pedro Silva
> Lupita Nyong'O
> William Saafir – Foreword to 'All My Men'
> Chuck Spady – Cover Graphics Designer
> Bobby Smith – Graphic Artist/IT

We all have special people who will inspire us to move beyond our self-imposed limitations. Sometimes these precious gifts are unaware of the value they bring to others. As with these individuals. It was something I read or gleaned from their writing that gave me hope or made a truism more real.

I play tribute to these and many others who have shown up for me throughout my life. So many I say proudly that a volume would be necessary to name them all. I listen and learn from all I interact with, be it a child, adult, homeless or disabled. Each person is worthy of honor and respect. Loving you where you are.

We hope you IN-joyed this Peace of Heaven book. Sandy Rodgers' intentions are to always uplift and encourage. She seeks to support people in thinking and living outside of the imaginary 'box' we have believed for too long to be our limitations.

Within the pages of this manuscript may you have discovered a phrase or story that will lead you to your place of authenticity of Pure Magic and total acceptance with unconditional Love for who you are and who you are destined to become.

Life is relatively short to miss any portion by believing you are less than or unworthy of any good and decent thing you may desire. The hope and prayer is that you learn to trust the process of life and of a Higher Consciousness that delivers you to a place of certainty that what you see in your mirror is Perfection and a godly Creation.

Bless you with the manifestation of your deepest desires and aspirations. If you would like more information about the writings of Sandy Rodgers please contact:

www.sandyrodgersministries.org
Sandy Rodgers Ministries Inc.
P.O. Box 67
Austell, GA. 30168
srm@sandyrodgersministries.org

Additional books by Sandy Rodgers:

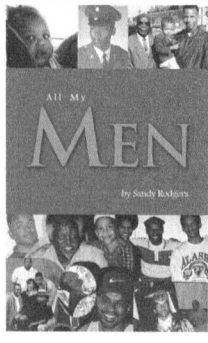

ALL MY MEN

THE ROSE GARDEN ...
remembering our beauty in tough times

WHEN GOD LEADS ...
just follow

And these book collaborations:

ERIEKA'S MAGICAL REALISM with H.E. Dr. EREIKA BENNETT

NATURAL HEALING: use Prayer, Food and Natural Healing as Natural Remedies with Imam William Saafir

Cornbread, Fish and Collards: Prayers, Poems & Affirmations for People Living with HIV/AIDS with Editor Khafre Kujichagulia Abif

All books are available at Amazon.com and www.sandyrodgersministries.org

REV. SANDY RODGERS

Affectionately known as "Mama Sandy" and "Sunshine" this Educator, Author, Minister, Certified NLP Life Coach and Reiki Master Teacher Practitioner shares her huge smile and her healing hugs with everyone she encounters.

In 2005, Rev. Sandy gave birth to the idea of marrying the New Thought Church with Holistic healing. This unprecedented union resulted in Rev. Sandy ushering in the modalities of Reiki, Breath-work, and the Dolphin Meditation to her global spiritual community. She is known as the "Mother of DAO" in the Atlanta DAO family.

Rev. Rodgers works lovingly within the communities of HIV/AIDS, DV/IPV (Domestic Violence and Intimate Partner Violence), women's rights and health, and overall community empowerment.

She distributes wisdom world-wide by producing and distributing her signature Daily IN-spirations and Health and Wellness blogs via the internet. Currently, Rev. Sandy is in the throes of creating audio files to heighten awareness around social topics and spiritual enlightenment.

With a lifelong pursuit of learning, community strengthening and multi-cultural sensitivity, Sandy Rodgers is professional, motivated, dependable, ambitious and focused on social reform while mastering interpersonal and leadership skills. She combines her spirituality with her corporate experience creating a unique blend of inspiring change by empowering people.

Rev. Rodgers' legacy of community service has been global in her efforts to outreach internationally. She began in 1993 by coordinating the USA-Berlin Initiative in Los Angeles bridging the divide of artists of various ethnic backgrounds to produce both music and an International Peace Mural in riot torn Los Angeles. She serves as the Matron of

African Heritage Youth Club in Ghana West Africa. She is organizer of the Total Wellness Project, addressing the psycho-social needs of children affected by AIDS in Africa, with a team of professionals across the United States.

Sandy works with the community to help people to understand the importance of proper nutrition. She is a certified Healing Foods Educator and teaches on the subject with each opportunity she sees. In so doing, she has developed courses for Baby Boomers that reminds this generation how eating can play a major role in their longevity. Her courses are called God's Groceries which includes a written blog.

Sandy is the esteemed radio personality of Life Love Wellness, The Sandy Rodgers Show.

My life purpose is to help people HEAL! Each action and interaction presents an opportunity to HEAL!

Follow Sandy Rodgers Ministries on Network Blogs @
http://Revsandy.wordpress.com for our daily inspirational blogs
http://twitter.com/MsSandy to follow us on Twitter
http://linkedin.com/RevSandy

**Listen in as we talk about subjects for
daily practical positive living ...
Weekly Radio: Tuesday Evenings 6pm PST / 9pm EST
www.http://blogtalkradio.com/
SandyRodgers/LifeLoveWellness
or call in 516-531-9819**

www.sandyrodgersministries.org

**Sandy Rodgers Ministries
P.O. Box 67, Austell, Georgia 30168
United States of America**

As for African American women, our mirror of beauty and acceptance has long been smashed into a million pieces, not just cracked .... *Sandy Rodgers*